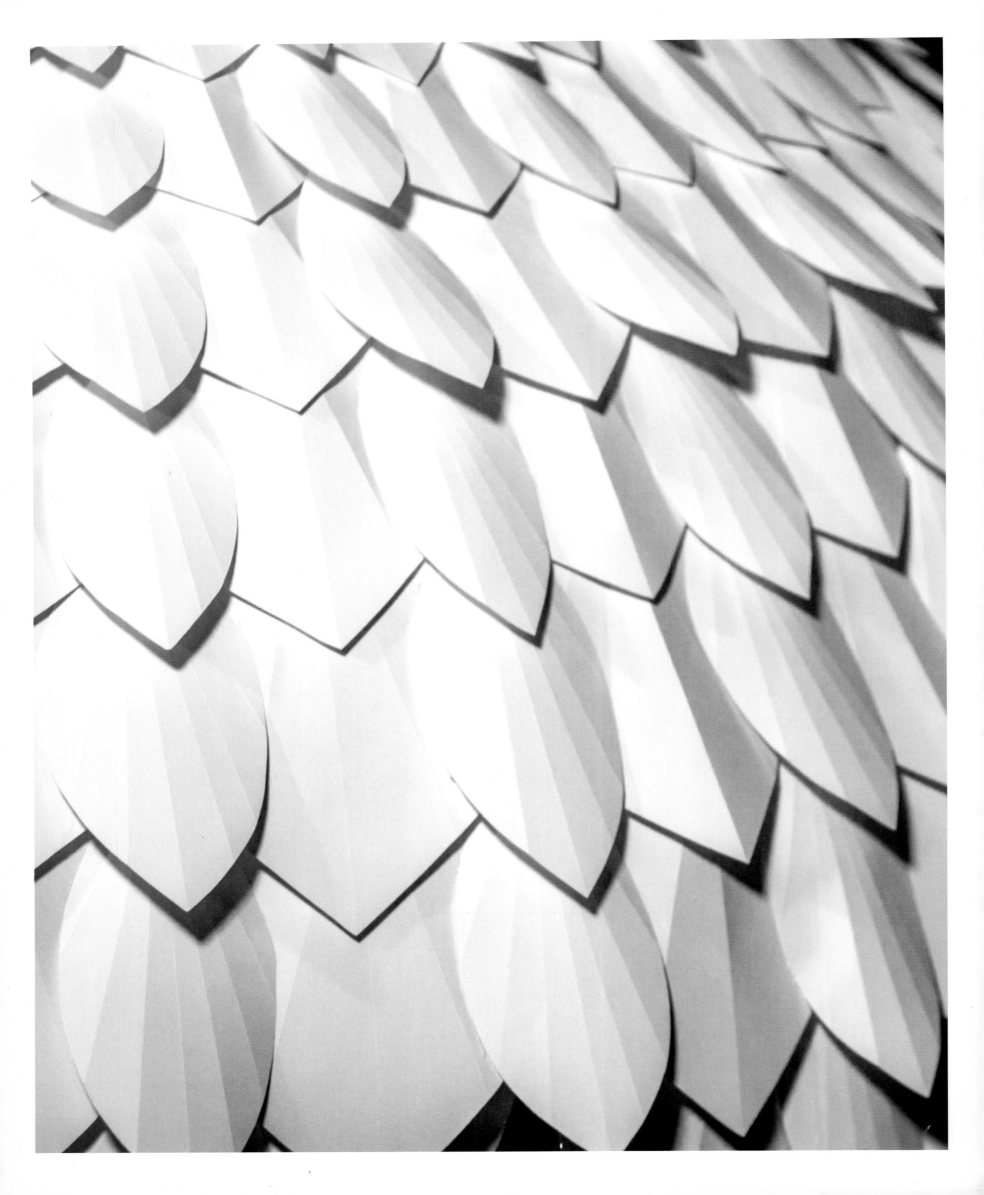

NEW CONTEMPORARY FASHION

EDITED AND DESIGNED BY
DANIEL "ATTABOY" SEIFERT

CERNUNNOS

INSIDE:

WEAR IT DOWN

PREFACE BY ATTABOY / *Hi-Fructose* Co-Founder

Sometimes form devours function and art overrides design. It mutates into something different. That's what this book is about. At least I think so.

My wife Annie and I started *Hi-Fructose Magazine* to present the blurred lines of the art world—we found excitement in the areas where various scenes and domains mingled and meshed. Or at least that's what we figured out, in hindsight many years later. Truth be told, we were just curious; and we knew what we liked. We knew how it felt to be "on the outs." The kitchen conversations that Annie and I have everyday have continually shaped what *Hi-Fructose* has become, and the same is true of the spirit and project of this book.

In these pages, we've gathered innovators, outliers, influencers, mutated misfits, and fashion icons in different transformative pupal stages.

In researching for this volume, I've found that beautiful doesn't have to be "pretty," at least in a traditional sense. And pretty can be so pretty that it becomes grotesque, and that... well, that can be quite beautiful, if convolutedly so. It's no surprise that this book includes more than a few designers who were inspired by the late Alexander McQueen's dark and elaborate constructions, and more so, the attitude that cuts across the usual lines.

I can't think of many things culturally that make people feel more alienated than the world of fashion, which is why it is so ripe for the exploration. This book might provide some evidence that there are true aliens amongst them.

Amidst the pomp and circumstance, there are really genuine creators pushing boundaries for more personal reasons than having a diluted ready-to-wear line at Barneys. They use wearable art as an obstant exclamation point, a (sometimes literary) suit of armor, or an impractical statement relegating its human host to a conversation sculpture that happens to breathe.

I tried to find designers that were showing their plumage without telling us onlookers what we "should" be wearing. I found many that want to share the joy of creation and that seem to revel in what they were doing, for a vast variety of reasons. Fancy, loud ensembles can be interesting, but what about the designers themselves? Many in this book aren't strictly concerned with the surface, but present a conversation with their art. What if the go-to

Hi-Fructose writers delved into this area?

They might reveal the absurdity of a catwalk experience, or, like Henrik Vibskov, create spectacles verging on performance art rather than using humans as mere models. They transplant the fashion experience to a drag strip or an environ more akin to a slaughterhouse. You'll find that many of their works are directly informed by their personal histories, traumas, and experiences.

They use new materials, the latest technology, or, like Enid Almanza, whatever-the-holy-heck they can get their hands on from the garage or hardware store. Whatever it takes to scratch that itch and transform themselves and others into a new, different state. Some of the creators in this book might be better described as sculptors, or technologists, or folk fetishists, or futurists, or simply costume designers. Pretty much anything other than traditional designers. I found former scientists, activists, circus performers, and do-it-yourself visionaries.

Like most things, the best tasting parts are toward the edges, where the shadows provide extra cover for ripening, where most don't care to make the effort to properly label.✦

HYPER COUTURE

INTRODUCTION BY ALINA CAMPBELL / Lucas Museum of Narrative Art Costume Archivist

I s fashion art? Conceptual fashion usually starts with art—inspiration from idea to sketch—which is transformed into a useful object. Influences, materials, and processes guide each designer on their path to creating each piece. *Hi-Fructose New Contemporary Fashion* contains impressive examples of art as fashion and vice versa. Through the lens of contemporary art, the *Hi-Fructose* editors have compiled fantastic examples from current cutting edge designers. Avant-garde designers push boundaries, they deconstruct and reconstruct fashion into unorthodox creations. This innovative group's take on contemporary design foreshadows the future of fashion and often shocks and challenges the viewer. Using unconventional materials, high-tech processes, and far-flung inspirations, they produce visionary fashion as wearable art.

The pinnacle of the fashion world is *Haute Couture*, or high fashion, where fashion is elevated to art. The term also translates to high sewing, or high dressmaking: custom handmade garments created to fit a specific client, made by the most skilled artisans and often constructed out of textiles created at the designer's request. *Haute Couture* houses have highly experienced ateliers, or workshops, of patternmakers, sewers and embroiderers—teams that transform a designer's vision to reality. *Haute Couture* handwork combined with the addition of new technology and innovation brings a new language into the development of fashion, transforming it and testing boundaries.

Haute Couture may aspire to fantastical, otherworldly ideals of beauty. Viktor & Rolf should be referenced because they consider themselves "Fashion Artists". They are unique examples of avant-garde *Haute Couture* fashion designers who bridge the gap between fashion and art. In their Autumn/Winter 2015 collection, fashion became wearable art as models were draped in large paintings that transformed into dresses. Viktor & Rolf's conceptual creations allowed them membership into the Parisian *Chambre Syndicale de la Haute Couture*—considered the highest honor from the most exclusive, invitation only, association in the fashion world. Only members of this elite organization are allowed to officially call their creations *Haute Couture*, and Victor & Rolf's sculptural designs have been collected and exhibited by museums with fashion collections across the globe.

Many of the designers in this book demonstrate innovative skills, have a deep understanding of *Haute Couture*, and each has a singular vision. One featured designer, Nicoline Liv Andersen, uses unconventional materials with the idea of "removing herself from the concept of functionality." These experimental garments, some not even wearable, challenge conventional notions of what fashion should be. Her aesthetic decidedly blurs the boundaries between art and fashion.

Transforming fashion into fluid, futuristic sculptures, Ana Rajcevic "calls into question our ideas about beauty and normality" by creating provocative body adornments that resemble bones and animal parts. Creating one-of-a-kind textiles using 3-D technology and digital

"THESE DESIGNERS DEFY TRADITIONAL IDEAS OF BEAUTY AND EXPAND THE BOUNDARIES OF ACCEPTABLE FASHION..."

manipulation, designers like Noa Raviv transform shapes into biomorphic, wearable garments that are both sculpture and fashion.

Sasha Frolova's inflatable latex body sculptures reinvent body shapes and borrow from Pop Art's vivid colors and bold shapes. Frolova, referencing pop culture iconography, created a yellow blow-up latex version of Princess Leia's iconic hair buns. Her work recalls legendary London club performance artist Leigh Bowery who played with body proportions and modifications to transform himself into a living, walking piece of art. Frolova often accompanies her silhouettes with huge, blow-up balloon sculptures to match the outfits, the juxtaposition creating an art installation atmosphere allowing the audience to visit.

Avant-garde fashion designer Kansai Yamamoto uses traditional Japanese Kabuki imagery in his iconic designs. He is best known for designing visionary outfits worn by David Bowie for his science fiction fantasy stage performances. During Bowie's *Ziggy Stardust* and *Aladdin Sane* tours, Yamamoto

created out-of-this-world glam rock garments. Playing with volume and Japanese aesthetics—especially noted in his "Tokyo Pop" bodysuit constructed out of vinyl with contrasting white stitching—his futuristic theatrical vision helped Bowie develop his alter ego.

Throughout the book, we see how manipulation of unusual materials is part of the design process. Manmade elements such as fiberglass, metal, resin, LED lights, and rubber are employed by some of the designers, while others transform "humble materials" such as cotton, wool and paper into the extraordinary. Utilizing digital 3-D sculpting to mimic handmade lace, designer Flavia Rose says, "The final object has more resonance and authenticity for me than when it is handmade." Others, like Anouk Wipprecht, use joints for movement and alien-like braided bones to create designs that alter the human form. We witness imagination on hyperdrive.

Details from some of these inventive designs could perhaps find their way into mainstream fashion with traditional fashion

designers always looking to these artful innovators for inspiration. In the future, we may see Olga Noronha's intricate gold lace ruffs worn around necks, or observe highly embellished work similar to Agnieszka Osipa's strutting down the street. One day we may even 3-D print our own sculptural clothing influenced by Bea Szenfeld. These designers defy traditional ideas of beauty and expand the boundaries of acceptable fashion, calling into question, *What is beauty? What is art? What is fashion?* According to the most well-known avant-garde fashion designer, the late, great Alexander McQueen, "Fashion should be a form of escapism and not a form of imprisonment."✦

BY ANDY SMITH

*I*t was only months before our conversation that Mirco Hepburn Arena graduated from the prestigious Polimoda Institute in Italy. Yet the Florence-based designer already knows what he wants to do in fashion, and it's a balance of ideas he's been pursuing since childhood. "I have always been fascinated by the fashion world and art in general," he says. "Every collection is a combination of research and emotions. In particular, in my collection *Dethroned Love*, I decided to tell my constant struggle between passion and rationality. I focused my attention on human instinct of seeking pleasure in what makes us suffer, which leads irredeemably to [a] 'freeze' of human relationships."

Dethroned Love is perhaps the best representation of the mix of "research and emotions" to date. There are the cold, protruding shapes adorning the faces of his models. And his headpieces and clothing, both jarring and transparent, reflect the complexity and intimacy found in Arena's so-called "dethroned love." He explains more of the intellectual side of that "freezing" effect and how it comes through in his work: "As water crystallized itself to become ice, transparent hues reinforce the cold and ethereal aura of the collection; plastic materials turned into geometric structures help recreating the fragility of snowflakes, while the shades of pink and nude tones represent the most intimate and passionate side of the human being," he offers. Further inspiration comes from the Sami, one of the indigenous tribes from Norway, with "the embroidery of skulls" representing rituals.

Arena is able to pull this off with a mix of materials. He mostly uses leather, "classical male wardrobe materials and more delicate ones" such as *organza*—a thin, sheer fabric. He then embellishes with crystals and pearls or by "using other techniques like lace applications on tulle." (Tulle is a lightweight netting.) Much of the shape of the objects is found in process, he says, which can vary wildly in duration. "I am really interested in tailoring pattern making so I spend the majority of the time trying to create the perfect shape I have in my mind," he says. "It can be just a day or even a week till the garment is perfect in my standards."

When asked if any of that leaves room for spontaneity, the designer maintains that "fashion is spontaneity. Spontaneity is the motor of life and what makes our lives more easy to live." It's his intentional study of the garment and materials that facilitates the ability to improvise alongside careful planning, he says. When he's prepared enough, he says, "simply, emotion flows."

A look at Arena's work—and an accompanying conversation—reveal an artist who revels in both vulnerability and confidence. And as his career is just beginning, he's able to move forward aware of the dualities existing throughout his chosen profession. "I am a combination of fragility and strength, so I often put what I feel inside in my work," Arena says. "And I am always open to dialogues with different [cultures'] life experiences and feelings that I translate into shapes and decorations."+

All photographs by Niccolò Chimenti.

MIRCO HEPBURN ARENA

"I AM A COMBINATION OF FRAGILITY AND STRENGTH, SO I OFTEN PUT WHAT I FEEL INSIDE MY WORK."

JO COPE

BY CARO

Jo Cope is an English designer who has been working at the intersection of fine art, fashion, design, and craft for over a decade. Her intriguing work is described as transcending the boundary of fashion, existing somewhere between design, fine art, and clothing—often coined as "hybrid installations." It involves impossible garments that when placed in an art gallery becomes wearable in our imagination. "I don't really think of them as hybrids but of course they are," Cope says. "Any relationship to hybrids is accidental it's the natural evolution of pushing fashion to a further point."

Currently based in Leicester, England, Cope is dedicated to re-defining the word "wearable" to mean "embodied." She believes that wearable fashion doesn't necessarily have to be practical. Her aesthetic is future facing, experimental, and minimalist all at once. Among her most circulated works are her formations of shoes stretched and bent like Gumby into conceptual arrangements. The colors are bright and vivid to those that convey a sense of earthiness, influenced by the work of Verner Panton and Pierre Cardin in the '60s and '70s. "I have an ongoing obsession with red, this is dominant over any other colors I have used," Cope shares.

"I am creating fashion where references to trend are often derived from social change. Even when the work looks more like art, it is still in tune with fashion's future and clothing trends in that moment; the red stiletto of last season would be an example of this." Her series, *The Language of Feet in the Walk of Life*, a creative and dynamic reimagining of a common red stiletto, pushed shoe design to its limits.

Fashion in the context of a museum or an art gallery typically celebrates a retrospect. Cope presents her work as a sort of "future fashion"—forms to be viewed by an art audience in the present. "The work is intended for an art gallery space as a static or performed installation where it can be viewed and contemplated," she explains. Another example is her work, "Walking in Circles," constructed after Cope's own size-seven shoe, using new and traditional shoe making techniques.

Works like these begin as a storyboard, as if Cope were staging a production rather than an art object: "I always have very strong ideas about what I want and my end vision, so I story board everything and heavily direct any photographers I work with." Her choice of materials is equally unexpected; recent pieces are made primarily with wood and Milliput epoxy putty and leather for pliability. A lot of the wood is found and recycled or repurposed. "My mind's eye is always the truest guide in visualizing what is meant to be created next, it is the way I interpret abstractly my life and experiences personally and of the world at any given point," she says.

A more recent piece is a dress cut to fit the body in a "fatal" floor position entitled "The Death of Love." This dress can be worn or embodied both in its flatness and also standing up, where it takes on a new and surprising form. When exhibited without a body, it becomes an installation object. Though made in the same way as a real dress, its intention as art is to carry emotion and hidden meaning for the designer:

"My original mission was to change people's perceptions of how fashion could exist and push the boundaries of fashion as a conceptual object. The caption that I would take to design shows was 'looking beyond what you already know in order to see differently.' A new piece I am working on at the moment is about metaphors for ambition and the ultimate commitment and connection to the self. Fashion, in my understanding of the word, is just inside me. I can't separate from it. Fashion in a non-commercial sense is a symbol of 'the others', the proportion of society in the minority that see the world differently."+

ABOVE: "Legs Open Eyes Shut". Photo by Nigel Essex.
OPPOSITE: "Formula Fashion Aerodynamic Dress". Photo by Derrick Kakembo.
1ST FOLLOWING SPREAD (L-R): "Formula Fashion Boots". Photo by Derrick Kakembo.
"Death of Love Dress". Photo by Nigel Essex.
2ND FOLLOWING SPREAD (L-R): "Looking for Love". Photo by Nigel Essex.

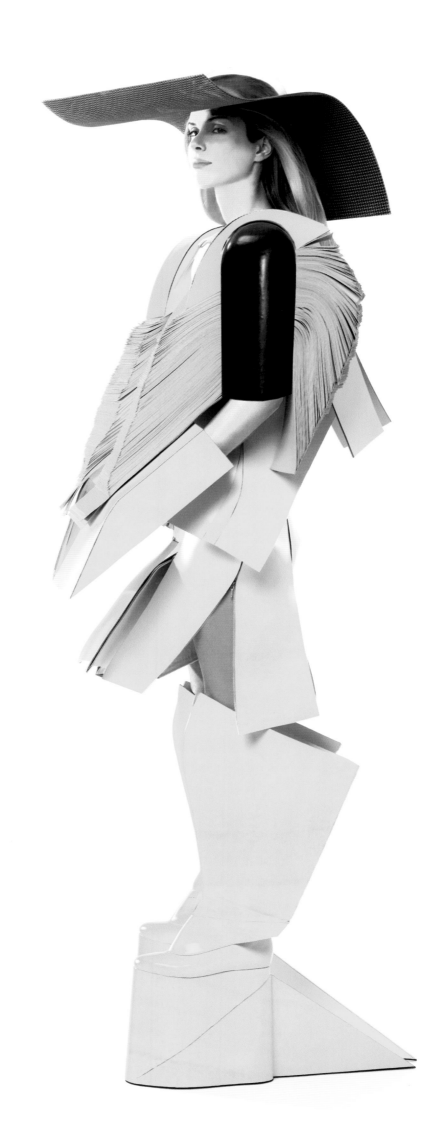

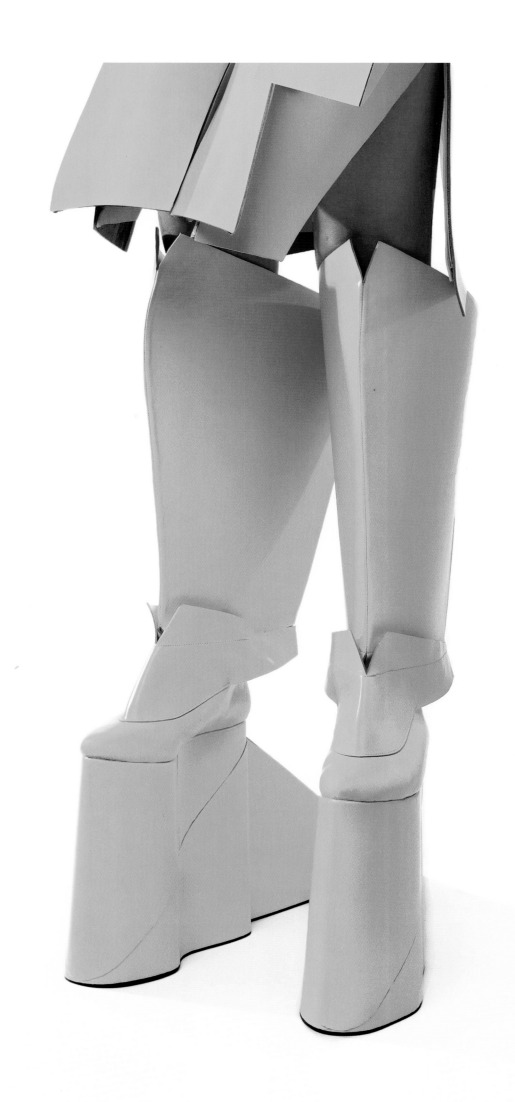

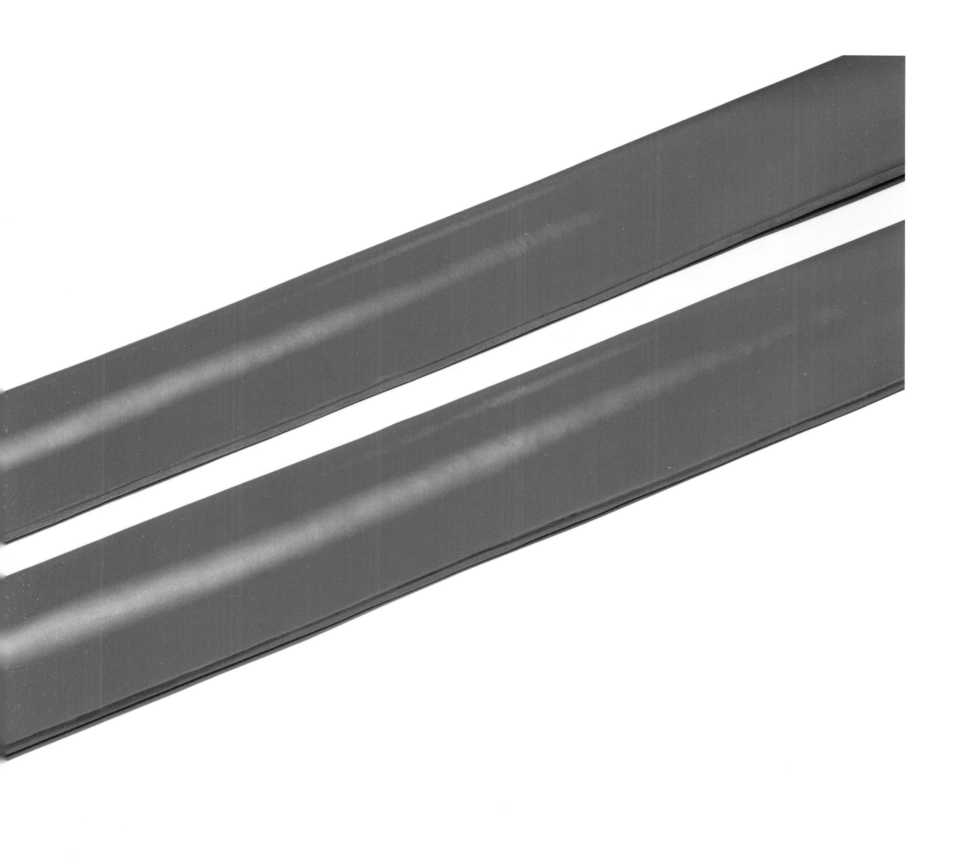

FLAVIA ROSE

BY ANDY SMITH

T he fields of costume design, wearable tech, photography, animation, film-making, graphic design, and propmaking may contribute to a single product, but it's not often you see one artist contribute to all of those trades. New Zealander Flavia Rose is a woman of many talents, and her wearable designs featured here benefit from analog and digital processes. "I love designing digitally for the freedom of having 'Ctrl+Z' and 'Save As', but I also love creating physical things for its inherent challenges and the satisfaction of creating something extraordinary from humble materials," Rose says. "The different skillsets complement each other well. I think my experience in creating physical objects gives me a good eye for detail and proportions in my digital work. And having digital skills means I don't feel stuck as a physical crafter with no way to move into the future."

And the artist is certainly progressing toward the future, with innovations in a series of "armours" and classical garments reimagined as immersive, light- and audio-filled clothing. Despite a startling output of wearable innovation, Rose doesn't actually have any formal training in costume design. Her undergrad was in film theory; her graduate work was under media design. She attended three different schools for these disciplines, moving between New Zealand and the U.K. Overall, she says, her academic background was a "very broad study in the visual communication of meaning." She's a storyteller, she says, and her garments relate a variety of narratives.

She takes this broad sensibility into Hollywood with her time at Weta Workshop, serving as a props technician on films like the live action version of *Ghost in the Shell*. During that same period, she toiled away on her own work, like the 2016 garment piece "Ester." That collaboration with Ashleigh-Jean King garnered a World of Wearable Art People's Choice Award and the VUW Visual Effects Society Award for "Creativity in Media Design."

"Ester" is a feminine, intricate dress using one thousand hand-cut paper petals and hundreds of NeoPixel LEDs. These lights can then be controlled

OPPOSITE: "Ester". Concept, design and paper craft by Ashleigh-Jean King and Flavia Rose, electronics and coding by Ashleigh-Jean King, cane sculpting by Flavia Rose. Hair and makeup by Victoria Hopgood, Modelled by Alexandra King, Supervised by Anne Niemetz, Victoria University of Wellington School of Design. "Ester" is handcrafted from cane and over a thousand hand-cut and etched paper petals. The garment is illuminated with three-hundred-forty Neopixel LEDs controlled by a Lilypad Arduino and is able to light up in an unlimited array of colors and behaviours. "These lights diffuse underneath the paper dress, allowing the garment to bloom, transforming it into a wearable light show."

ABOVE: "High Tide". Cane and vellum sculpting by Flavia Rose. Concept, design, sewing by Bianca Taylor. Electronics and coding by Ash King. Hair and Makeup by Courtney Taylor. Modelled by Henrietta Hitchings. Inspired by Ernst Haeckel's Art Forms in Nature, this seashell dress is a high fashion art piece. An MP3 Arduino Lilypad controls the functions of the garment–reacting to a light sensor; two speakers embedded in the shells produce ambient deep-sea music, when it senses that the external lights are dimmed. LED strips, hidden within the shell forms and neckline of the corset, react to the volume of the music thus submerging the viewer deeper into the atmospheric experience. "This piece is designed to encapsulate the wonder of the ocean. Through diffused light and soundscape. 'High Tide' inspires memories of rock pools and beach days in an elegant, glamorous new context."

"THERE IS A HUGE PROCESSION OF LIGHT, LANTERNS, AND PERFORMERS... THE CARNIVAL COMPLETELY ENCHANTED ME AND SEEDED A STRONG DESIRE TO MAKE OBJECTS AND GARMENTS LIGHT UP."

for any behavior or RGB color desires. And the result is a shocking, yet somehow elegant, vision of future fashion.

Rose's knack for blending the digital and the handmade don't end there. Her "Lace Armour," which comments on the "on the symbolic or emotional armour that women wear everyday," is partially made using 3-D printing, which broadly, has revolutionized wearable fashion and wearable tech. For Rose, the advent of 3-D printing hasn't been as much of a game-changer. "At the end of the day I'd rather handcraft something than print it, as the final object has more resonance and authenticity for me when it is handmade," she says. "I see 3-D printing more as a prototyping tool, a way to rapidly iterate upon an idea."

Using all of these technological tools does come with challenges. The three-hundred-forty LEDs on "Ester" were difficult to power. To combat voltage drop issues, "which caused our pure-white garment to light up as a Hellish red," Rose and company had to keep adding difficult-to-find Lithium Polymer batteries. Even if you have the right sizes of printer and materials, the most readily available 3-D

printers do have limitations for Flavia. Any raw plastic print, Rose says, needs much sanding, priming, refining, and painting. Overall, the hardships are numerous, but Rose and collaborators are able to overcome while pushing fields forward.

Rose attributes part of that drive to her native New Zealand. She says the diversity of her country's landscape "means inspiration is never far away." And the broader freedom creators receive makes that difference, too. Her "armours" are free to tackle social issues, and in particular the ever-present issues revolving around gender.

The "Lace Armour" is a nod to needlework and the traditional role of women in crafting. Rose injects femininity into a traditionally masculine tool for defense, thus pushing through viewers'—and bearers'—expectations. The "Embroidered Lace Armour" doesn't use the same 3-D printing tactics as the other "lace" creation. She implemented a Janome Memory Craft 9900 CAD embroidery machine for the task, inviting echoes of industrial revolution into the conversation. And yet another atypical garment of defense, the "Leaf Armour," brings mythology into the equation. Its pauldrons

---

OPPOSITE: "High Tide", detail.
ABOVE, LEFT: "Ester", work in progress of caning technique.
ABOVE, RIGHT: "3-D Printed Lace Armour". Concept, 3-D modelling, and 3-D printing by Flavia Rose. "This project on lace armour is a commentary on the symbolic or emotional armour that women wear everyday. The lace ties into notions of 'women's work', such as the needlework our great-grandmothers

would have spent hours handcrafting. The purpose of making lace into armour is to invest a traditionally masculine object (armour) with femininity, and to draw on the strength and power of something traditionally seen only for its beauty and fragility." Lace designed in Illustrator, extruded in Rhino, deformed in Maya, printed on an UP Box machine using ABS filament.

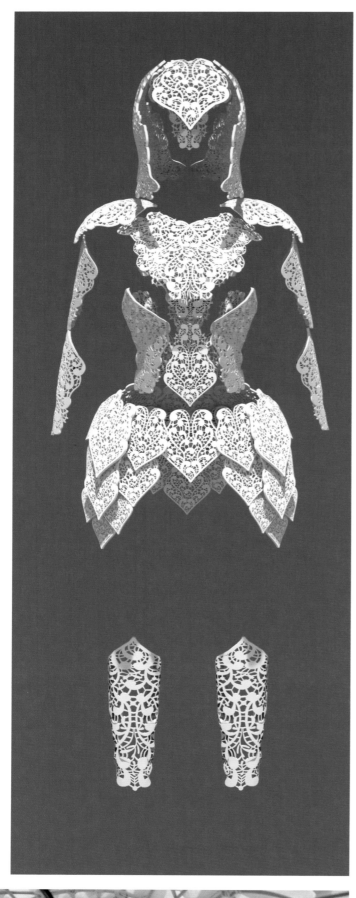

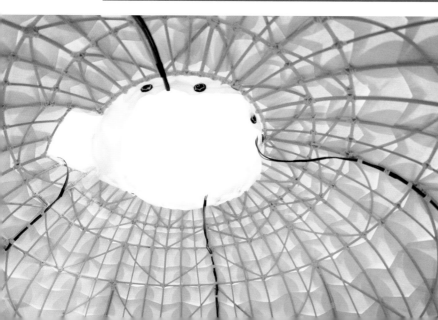

comes from a blending of handmade paper, camellia leaves, cotton thread, and cane. Artemis is the muse here, with the goddess's protection of the natural world and young girls at play.

Early on, she recalls, one of her biggest aesthetic influences was the Dunedin Midwinter Carnival in the South Island of New Zealand, which has been running for the past twenty years. "I grew up in Dunedin, where it is pretty cold and dark for most of the year," Rose says. "Each year, on the Midwinter Solstice, there is a huge procession of light, lanterns, and performers through the center of the city. The community gets involved in the making of the lantern parade, and artists make giant lanterns in fantastical shapes, like huge whales and peacocks, even a unicorn. I was involved in the Carnival from a young age and this is where I learned to craft cane, a skill I've used in many of my garments. The Carnival completely enchanted me and seeded a strong desire to make objects and garments light up."

She took this inspiration into these pieces, and additionally, into her 3-D animation shorts, documentaries, and graphic design projects. All of her endeavors seem to spill into each other. Each is the mark of an artist who can't stop making, whether through mouseclicks or sewing, 3-D printing or tiny cuts with scissors, school projects or major motion pictures.

The latter item in that list arrived only recently. "I learnt a lot during my time at Weta Workshop, not only how to correctly use a drill press," she remembers. "Previously I had worked on local film and TV productions, but being a props technician for *Ghost in the Shell* and [the most recent] *Power Rangers* was my first experience of a big budget Hollywood crew. The most important thing I took away from Weta was to think bigger; the workshop started off as a grassroots kiwi company and has become the biggest workshop of its kind in the world, a global player in costumes, weaponry, and practical effects."

On *Ghost in the Shell*, Rose's props and model contributions can be seen across the featured characters: Major Motoko Kusanagi's thermooptic suit, the chest prosthetic for Kuze, the hacking tongues on the Geisha, and various tech implants throughout. Her time on Power Rangers was marked by 3-D printing, costume assembly, and the odd, yet integral task of adding tiny cracks to each of the six suits seen in the film.

But what was her biggest lesson learned working with Weta? "If anything, it taught me that while our country may be small, our vision can be huge," Rose says.✛

OPPOSITE (CLOCKWISE FROM TOP): "Lace Armour" design progress, "Leaf Armour": Concept and handcrafting by Flavia Rose. Pauldron from cane, cotton thread, handmade paper and freshly picked camellia leaves. Inspired by the Greek goddess Artemis, goddess of the wilderness, the hunt, and the protector of young girls. Detail of "Leaf Armour" hand-crafting, "Embroidered Lace Armour": Concept, CAD, and handcrafting by Flavia Rose. Lace armour designed in Illustrator, created using a Janome Memory Craft 9900 CAD embroidery machine. "The purpose of the project was to explore the industrial revolution in the fashion industry and invest a traditionally masculine object (armour) with elements of femininity." Detail of skirt from "Ester".

ABOVE: Rose's "Ester" project in full glow.

ANA RAJCEVIC

BY ANDY SMITH

Alone, works by Ana Rajcevic are isolated reflections of the natural world. Yet, when the pieces are worn by models, each is activated—or as the artist says, "fused with the person"—in a way that the human body becomes an entirely new creature.

It's also how Rajcevic expresses her vision in both the world of fashion and the world of art. Any purported line between the two doesn't exist. "In my opinion, the strict border between art and design mediums is totally artificial and absurd, and I enjoy shifting experiences from one field to another," Rajcevic says. "It is all about visual communication of abstract values and ideas, and I use art as a language to communicate the things I care about. If we look at sculptural objects, they acquire an entirely different meaning when they are constructed in relation to the body. On the other hand, there's not an art that has a more immediate relationship with the body than fashion art. Both sculpture and fashion are visual fields, and they can refer to one another. In my work they kind of tend to morph into one."

The double nature of Rajcevic's work forces her output into descriptors like "wearable sculptures" or "body sculptures." This so-called multi-disciplinary dialogue is something long pursued by the artist/designer (who even shares a dual home—between Berlin and London). The University of the Arts London graduate has exhibited these pieces across the world, from the Louvre in France to the Smithsonian Design Museum in New York City. In that time, the awards have stacked up and

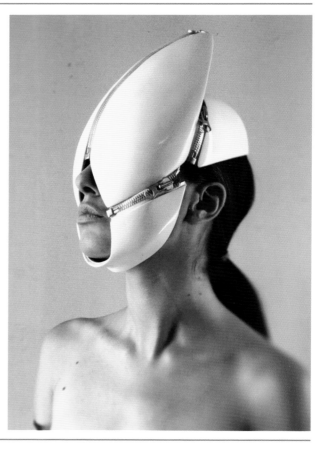

ABOVE: Animal: The Other Side of Evolution, wearable sculpture (wax, polyurethane, rubber, 2012). Photo by Fernando Lessa. Model: Anna Tatton. RIGHT: "YFF Piece." OPPOSITE: Animal: The Other Side of Evolution. Wearable sculpture (wax, polyurethane, rubber, 2012). Photo by Fernando Lessa. Model: Anna Tatton.

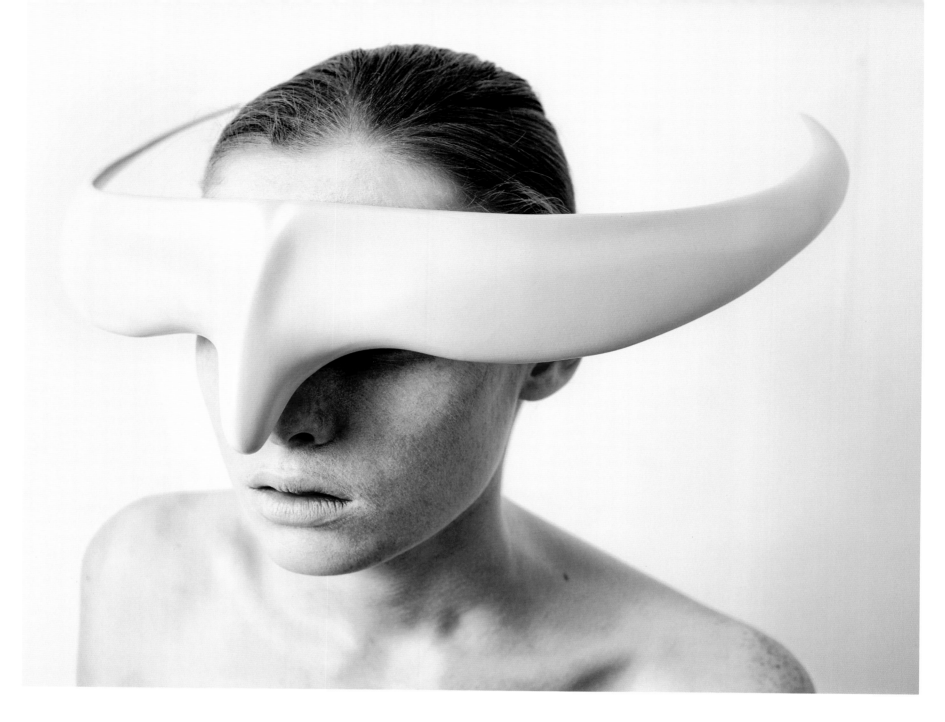

reflect her multiple disciplines: a 2013 SEED Award for Exceptional Talents, a British Global Award for "Artist of the Year," and the 2015 Outstanding Creation & Invention Prize at Biennale Internationale de Design, Saint Etienne. Lately, she's also had some unlikely collaborations: She's working with Neurobotics Research Lab in Berlin and Berlin University of the Arts research fellow Marco Donnarumma on an artificially intelligent robot, a human-like limb called "Amygdala." The project looks at the ties between robotics, art, and ritual performance. Elsewhere, she's working on a contemporary ballet piece with London's Neon Dance Company.

So, what's the through-line in the artist's practice? What's the engine of these multi-genre explorations? She distills it down to a word: "[in] my work I deal with the general idea of 'humanity,'" she explains. "By exploring the fluid concepts of identity construction and self-representation, I call into question our ideas about beauty and normality, human and non-human, relationships between the rational and the subconscious, the mind and the body. Through critical work in the form of 'prosthetic body-sculptures,' I question: What does it mean to be human today? What is abled-body in the twenty-first century?"

This led to the recent series *Animal: The Other Side of Evolution*. As the subtitle suggests, the collection deals with a fictional evolution, one in which humankind is more in-tune with and has evolved alongside nature. In this world, man is not so consumed with wealth and taking advantage of the animal kingdom and the Earth. The new possibilities from humankind immersing itself in the planet that birthed it is the basis of *Animal*. Perhaps ironically, the artist accomplishes this with manmade materials: fiberglass, polyurethane, and rubber. In general, the artist says she uses "mostly industrial and medical materials like silicones, silicon-rubbers, and polymers," which "are contemporary materials of great utility, predominantly made for industrial usage and medical devices that have contact with the human body." She says that the ability of these materials to move between solid and liquid forms, and between rigidness and a flexibility, make them appropriate for her projects.

The "organic" final result is a process of trial and error. She prepares with an immense amount of drawing, research, and experi-

"...WHAT WE PERCEIVE TODAY AS 'HUMAN' MIGHT BE SUBSTANTIALLY DIFFERENT THAN WHAT WE WILL EXPERIENCE IN DECADES TO COME."

mentation. "I'm really interested in the inter-linkages of art and science, and overlap between material research and technology," she adds. "I often work closely with material specialists, combining material innovation through physical form-finding experiments which helps me deepen my research and exploration of the topics."

The dialogue stirred by Rajcevic goes beyond fashion and art, technology and the natural world. In the end, she hopes her pieces create internal debates, one in which the viewer is able to question his or her own place in the world. It's a lofty goal—to use such alien and surreal imagery to create such a profoundly personal result. "The question of animality touches upon all concepts and questions of humanity," she maintains. "Which human being is simply human? Where does the animal begin and where does it end? How is this unity and separation problem of man and animal reflected in today's idea of human? Is it really possible isolating such an essential core of man? I believe that what we perceive today as 'human' might be substantially different than what we will experience in decades to come."✦

PREVIOUS SPREAD and THIS SPREAD: Animal: The Other Side of Evolution, *wearable sculpture (wax, polyurethane, rubber, 2012). Photos by Fernando Lessa. Model: Anna Tatton.*

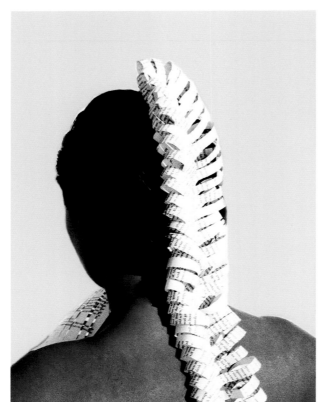

STEVEN VANDERYT

BY ANDY SMITH

Dutch designer Steven Vanderyt has described his pieces as "raw, provocative, and feminine." His couture pieces are designed to endure, untethered to a specific time or year and organized simply under labels like Season 1 or Season 2. This is Vanderyt's "slow-fashion" approach to exclusive pieces, abandoning the concept of trendiness and attempting to inject longevity into each ensemble.

Each "season" has brought the world something different. Season 7, titled *Ogeretla*, tackles the internet culture and "gives a take on these desperate ways on living that online glamour life by pieces who lose their function and are used to create manipulated silhouettes." Season 5, titled *2DIE4*, examined Chinese death rituals and the custom of "hell money," paper resembling actual money that's burnt after a loved one's death to give them currency in the afterlife. In this collection, the models are preparing to enter heaven wealthy, adorned with paper.

All of these projects hint at Vanderyt's stated mantra: "The mission is to keep on surprising or shock with my approach to fashion and by doing so, also inspire others to always celebrate creativity and freedom," he says, in a statement. "With my experimental design with low-culture elements mixed with high-end craftsmanship with a couture touch, [this] gives quite an original view on fashion. I like to tell stories with my collections. I take global or social problems and I romanticize these problems, give them a layer of fantasy. To really make my stories complete I transform outfits into characters to

give them a setting in the story, to give the story a more personal approach, that something that the viewer can relate to."

2DIE4 was chosen by the high-end department store De Bijenkorf to be shown at one of their major in-store events. That happened when the designer was in his third year at School for the Arts Utrecht. He graduated a year after that and unveiled *Couture De Jour* (Season 6). It was his statement against "the system." From his statement:" Let couture be art, not fashion. He started working with the idea to make sculptures without somebody wearing the piece. To make his own models and make the garment around the model, so the model would be trapped in the garment."

The fashion world took notice, with award nominations and invitations to fashion week events in London, Vancouver, and Shanghai. The designer's noted that his mission is also to "conquer the world with my designs and to share with the world my view on design." It seems as though he's getting his chance.✛

ABOVE (L-R): "Skeletor". Model: Nina Gerritsen. Photo by Steven Vanderyt.
OPPOSITE: Backstage at the FC17 Fashion Show.
1ST AND 2ND FOLLOWING SPREADS: Shots from the FC17 Fashion Show.

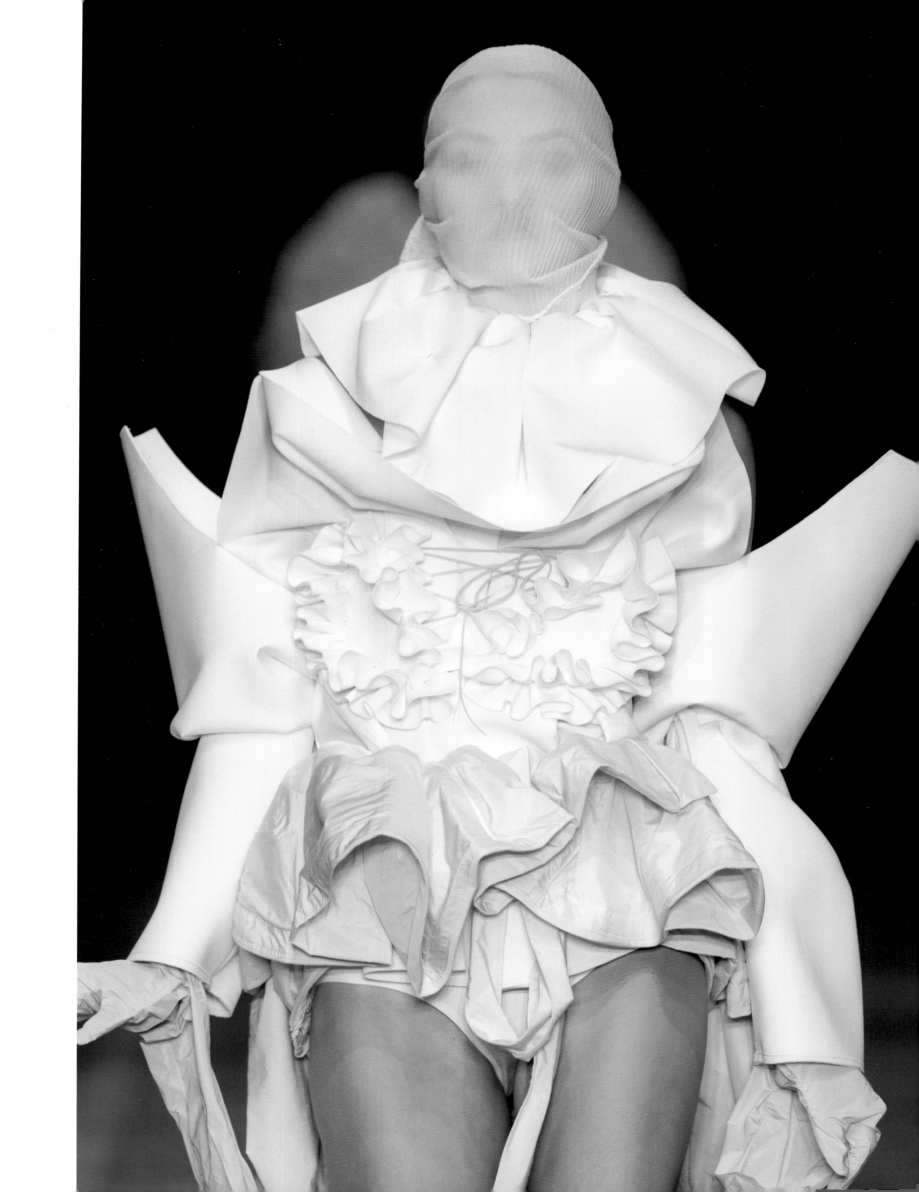

VERONIKA RABINOVICH

BY ANDY SMITH

There's a whimsical quality to the vibrant, human-animal hybrid creatures created by New York City-based artist/designer Veronika Rabinovich. Perhaps this is why her website is given the title of *Dream Caverns*, a place where the strange and surreal are embodied by her endearing, yet slightly unsettling costumes and puppets. Rabinovich points to her earliest memories as an influence: "I was born in Russia, and when I was child, I listened to old Russian fairytale records," she recalls. "These fairytales have influenced my path from drawing and sculptures into costume. Also, being involved in theater and dance helped the evolution of my work."

The St. Petersburg-born designer moved to Brooklyn with her parents, sister, and grandparents in 1981. She later graduated from New York's School of Visual Arts in 1999, before garnering more and more attention for her costumes.

Among Rabinovich's influences today are films, theatrical productions, music, and dance. In cinema, it's the work of names like Jean Cocteau, Alejandro Jodorowsky, Emir Kusturica, and David Lynch that inspire Rabinovich to push further into the territory of surrealism. You can see traces of these filmmakers' works in Rabinovich's costumes, echoes of Lynch's *Rabbits* or Cocteau's titular beast in *Beauty and the Beast*. There's both an earnest formality to their apparel and unabashed absurdity to their faces and expressions.

> THERE'S BOTH AN EARNEST FORMALITY TO THEIR APPAREL AND UNABASHED ABSURDITY TO THEIR FACES AND EXPRESSIONS.

OPPOSITE: Pandgnatious out on the town. Photo by Mario Lobo.
ABOVE: Rabinovich at work in her studio in Weehawken, New Jersey.
Photo by Michael Mundy.

The Characters of Dream Caverns

DR. TRANSFUSSION: "The creator of the magical world of animals and musical instruments." (SEE FOLLOWING SPREADS)

ADMIRAL SNIFTER: "The Admiral plays the trumpet in the morning and makes other animals dreams come true." (SEE FOLLOWING SPREAD)

CROCMADILLO: "The reverend is half armadillo half crocadile who is a religious character, performs festive ceremonies." (SEE FOLLOWING SPREAD)

"PANDGNATIOUS is a character who expresses himself through zen and tai-chi, spiritual and a philosophical being." (SEE PREVIOUS SPREAD)

"WULFCHALLOWSKY is an intricate wolf who plays the violin and performs during full-moon nights with lightning bugs." (OPPOSITE, TOP LEFT)

"KAKKLE DOODLE DOO is a Polish chicken who plays the banjo while making cackle sounds during poultry meetings." (OPPOSITE, TOP RIGHT)

"PROFESSOR INGO is a distinguished magician who calls attention with the xylaphone." (OPPOSITE, BOTTOM RIGHT)

"PURRTASTIC is a Korean drummer who purrs and meows while playing drums; a multiskilled feline." (BELOW, LEFT)

"TAILOR RING is a coquettish lemur who plays jazzy tunes on her piano. She often goes back in time to the 1920s." (BELOW, RIGHT)

"PORCUCORN is a hedgehog who counts insects while playing an instrument called a balalaika." (OPPOSITE, BOTTOM LEFT)

THIS SPREAD: All photos by Mario Lobo.

OPPOSITE: Crocmadillo out in the world. Photo by Mario Lobo.
ABOVE: Admiral Snifter plays a song , while Dr. Transfussion eggs him on.
Photo by Mario Lobo. BELOW, TOP: Wulfchallowsky in the snow. Photo by
Scott Irvine. BELOW, BOTTOM: Dr. Transfussion and his mighty whip.
Photo by Mario Lobo.

"MY GOAL IS TO PRODUCE A FILM OR PERFORMANCE... TO PUT OUT A MESSAGE OF HUMANITY'S ENDLESS POSSIBILITIES IN THE FACE OF OBSTACLES..."

Today, it's not uncommon to see her characters at events like Scope Art Fair in Miami, milling about and delighting fellow gallery-goers. You might find Reverend Crocmadillo, the warrior Pandgnatious, the owl-headed Admiral Snifter, or even Porcucorn, a porcupine-like creature covered in acorns. The characters all seem to be pulling from differing mythologies and cultures around the world, with the common thread of influence being the natural world and the designer's irreverent humor. Each character's jaunt through a cultural event is a piece of performance art, the part of Rabinovich's process in which her creations becoming living beings. And the artist herself is often the one adorned with the costumes.

As for the process that precedes that part of a character's journey, Rabinovich says it all starts "with a rough sketch, and from there, a structural form is built." It may take two months or a year to build one of her characters. And when they begin to take shape, "the decorative part is where it turns spontaneous."

These builds occur between projects for the designer, who also has puppetry, painting, and food-styling practices. (The food is the most removed from her usual whimsy, though she calls it "another medium I use for self-expression.") One gets the sense that with each of her characters, though, Rabinovich is constructing something larger—a place mischievous and fantastical that's slowly merging with our own.

When asked what her eventual goal is, she offers: "My main project is the world I am creating with the costumed characters," she says. "My goal is to produce a film or performance with all the characters. And with these characters to put out a message of humanity's endless possibilities in the face of obstacles, and there is unique place for everyone."✦

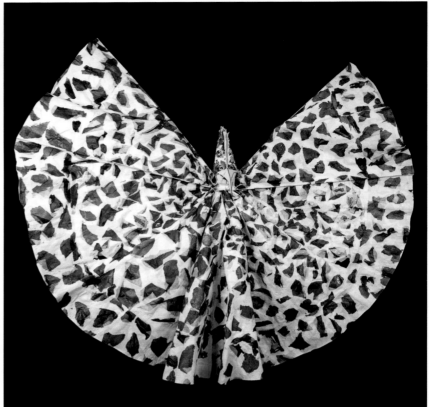

TIEL JANSEN

BY ANDY SMITH

First comes an idea, a pencil, and an open mind, says Netherlands designer Tiel Janssen. Next, a reduced scale—a 1:6 model—where the artist tests "the influence of the materials, the light intensity, the color effect, and the abstract feeling is sought, which is expressed in materials and shapes." And then, it's time for a full-scale test.

In its most distilled terms, that's the process of this celebrated designer of wild costumes and jewelry that transform models into fantastical characters. The phrases most often associated with Janssen's work are "wearable art" or "portable" art. Many of the materials she uses are "self-developed," using plastics and other recycled sources to create something new. The two- to three-month process of creating one costume occurs in three levels, but as she tells me, every work is actually forged with three concepts: "the body as a carrier, nothing is normal and everything is special."

And each point along the way comes with its own challenges. The second stage with a small model is where the broader idea behind the concept is first truly tested. And Tiel offers this on the third point in her process, when her theatrical costume begins to become life-sized: "This is a new challenge due to the characteristics of materials, colors, spatial operation and patterns," she says. "The first concept is central and is approached as shortly as possible. It is important to keep alert to the relationship between material and color and mutual cooperation of light and composition to achieve the right result—and that is the abstract feeling."

The results are massive, living sculptures that can appear as moving mosaics or a human-shaped carnival game. At times, they appear plucked from ancient festivals; elsewhere, they seem on slightly human. When asked where she looks for inspiration outside of the world of fashion, Janssen says "there is no affinity with the fashion world." Instead, Janssen's work relies on a combination of life experience and the world that surrounds her. "The inspiration and motivation lies in the characteristics of personal development related in the context of the past, present and future," she says. "Current issues may also play a role, such as environmental protection or recycling of raw materials."

The designer's background is in both what she calls "autonomous textile education" at Academy of Textile Arts in Belgium and the Academy for Theater Costume Design in Maastricht Netherlands. "The creations lie between the 'autonomous' and the application of 'theater costume design,' because an autonomous image is static and a theater costume is subordinate to the actor. The open mind and the development of new materials [remain important]." Today, Janssen's vision has garnered her recognition in New Zealand's international 2017 World of WearableArt Awards.

And though she's honed a style referenced above in three distinct stages, there's always room for surprise. When you're working with self-developed materials, something spontaneous is bound to happen. "This can occur during the work process from the design to the finished product, the costume," she says. "The designer must remain open and see this as a gift that could not have been dealt with beforehand."✦

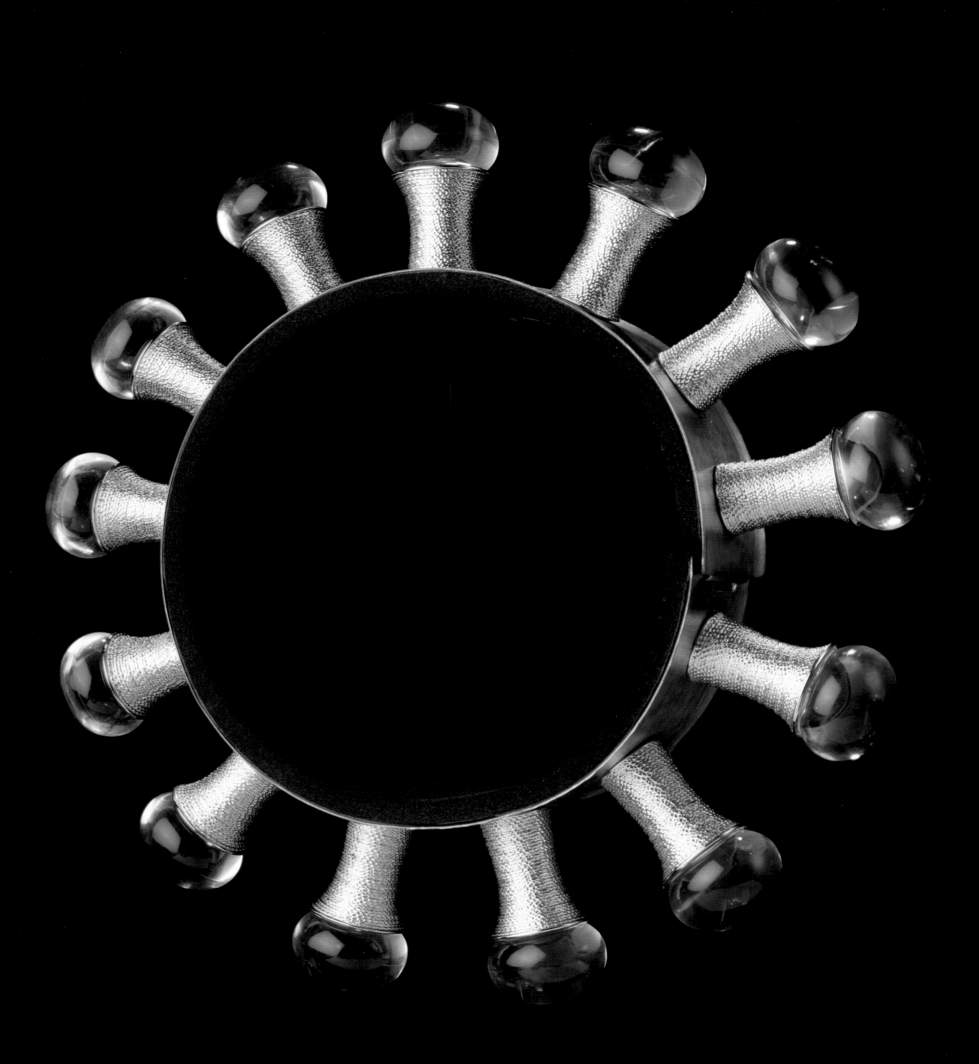

JILLIAN OLIVER

BY SILKE TUDOR

Named for a vengeance demon from *Buffy the Vampire Slayer*, the "Anya Bonnet" strikes a slightly deeper psychological chord the first time you see Jillian Oliver wearing it. The hat is soft, a crocheted chimera shaped like a flight helmet—hugging her face and fastened under the chin, with long, soft bunny ears falling past her shoulders. Oliver stands in a gray, concrete room. Her dark eyes stare off-camera into nothing; her slight body is encased in a bodice of restraint straps laid over a soft, heather-gray jumper. The "Ezri Jumper" is sexy, clinging to every dip and curve of Oliver's frame, with hot pants and a peek-a-boo cutout. But it's very wrong. The arms stretch nearly to the floor like a straightjacket, making the principal allusion to insanity impossible to ignore.

The juxtaposition between huggable and horrible, sexy and uncanny, is not unusual for Oliver. A lover of sci-fi and psychological horror, Oliver will create bondage belts and gimp masks—made of soft fabrics but nightmarishly cock-eyed—to accessorize a sprightly A-line mini-dress, or a crocheted crop-top with bell sleeves. Body-hugging shifts, made of the most inviting jersey, are riddled with cutouts that are more manic than suggestive. Huge stitches run across skirts and cozy leggings like sutures. *Bandeaus* consist of strips of white fabric, wrapped like bandages across the chest. The intimation of trouble—both internal and external—inhabit many of Oliver's designs; and yet, the clothes are undeniably precise, beautifully fitted, and meticulously sewn.

OPPOSITE: From the Sheath Collection. Photo by Hana Haley. Model: Jillian Oliver.
ABOVE: From the Sheath Collection. Photos by Olin Caprison. Model: Jillian Oliver.

"I AM COMPLETELY SELF-TAUGHT," SAYS OLIVER. "WITH EVERY PROJECT I DO, I LEARN HOW TO MAKE MY WORK BIGGER AND BETTER."

"I started the brand, making clothes for myself," explains Oliver.

It's difficult to imagine Oliver stomping around her hometown like a ghostly version of Tank Girl, wearing knee-high platform sneakers, a white aviator helmet, and lace-up halter top with crocheted hot pants. Even an earlier, more sedate ensemble—say, a high-necked '60s-style shift with buckled leggings, missing at the knees—would better complement a crewmember on the *Enterprise* than a denizen of a small burg in the Sierra Nevada foothills.

"I grew up feeling completely stifled by my environment," admits Oliver. "The culture was sheltered, and any deviation was met with extremely harsh ridicule. High school was an absolute nightmare for me."

As a consequence, Oliver didn't begin to take her talents seriously until she moved to Los Angeles when she was thirty. There, a photographer pal insisted on shooting the clothes she had made to wear, as a collection.

Since then, Oliver has been employed as a costumer for Disney Style, as well as a costume fabricator for the musician Peaches. She has designed clothes for Violence, Sigur Rós, and Thirty Seconds to Mars, and she has provided Brazilian performance artist Lilian Colosso with sleeves so long they could encircle a grove of trees. All the while, the world of Sheath has expanded.

"I am completely self-taught," says Oliver. "With every project I do, I learn how to make my work bigger and better."

Seemingly inspired by futuristic cosmonauts, Elizabethan garden parties, and graphic novels like *The League of Extraordinary Gentlemen*, the latest Sheath collection is presented, like almost all of Oliver's designs, in achromatic white. Oliver's face, done up like a deranged porcelain baby doll, stares out from beneath a flouncy bonnet, petal-shaped *cloche*, sophisticated halo, and a newly designed starfighter helmet. Large ruffs for the neck, wrists, or ankles add either an outlandishly royal or disturbingly clownish flare, depending on posture and intent. Thigh-high spats complement a *bandeau* made of straps. Highly exaggerated jodhpurs are met by the similarly ballooning sleeves of a Bolero jacket or the skeletal suggestion of a halter-top. The "Ziyal Suit"—named no doubt for a Cardassian/Bajoran character on *Deep Space Nine*—features a wildly exaggerated scalloped edge, much like an alien clavicle, running the length of the sleeves and pant legs. Beautifully crafted springtime Macs and reinforced, battle-ready pedal pushers give way to the flounce of a deconstructed flamenco dress and a similarly denuded miniskirt.

Despite the high-summer incorruptibility of the crisp, white cotton used for this collection, Sheath's clothes are made to be worn—if not to survive any number of probable apocalypses. (A little blood and grubbiness around the seams will only enhance their distinctive allure.) Stewing on tales by H.P. Lovecraft and reruns of *The Twilight Zone* while Oliver sews will probably give her just the right idea for fighting Cthulhu.✦

OPPOSITE: From the Sheath THR3E Collection. *Model: Jillian Oliver.*
ABOVE: From the Sheath Collection. *Photo by Hana Haley. Model: Jillian Oliver.*
1ST FOLLOWING SPREAD (LEFT): From THR3E, *Photos by Ian Miyawaki and Hana Haley.* 2ND FOLLOWING SPREAD (LEFT): From the Sheath THR3E Collection. *Model: Jillian. Oliver (RIGHT): Photo by Hana Haley. Model: Jillian Oliver.*

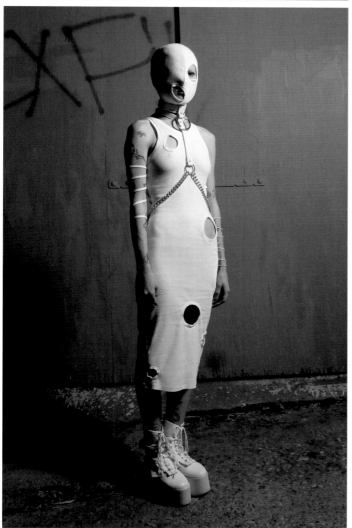

HENRIK VIBSKOV

BY ANDY SMITH

Henrik Vibskov is not only a creator of garments, but of new worlds for each to inhabit. The work of this Danish fashion designer, often association with the "New Nordic Movement" of contemporary, eclectic artists, wholly contrasts with Scandinavian minimalism. Instead, accompanying the clothes are "a multitude of twisted yet tantalising universes created in relation to each collection," a statement says.

The Jutland native—a graduate of Central Saint Martins College of Art and Design in London—is notable enough in the world of garments. His products are worn by members of Sigur Rós and LCD Soundsystem, Lou Reed, M.I.A., Björk, and Devendra Banhart. He's produced more than thirty men's collections (and further into his career, women's collections too), has been a Paris Men's Fashion Week staple since 2003. The work has brought him to festivals, competition, runways, and jury positions across the world and is sold through shops, including his own in Copenhagen and New York.

But it's in a Vibskov-produced show that his vision and sense of humor truly shines. In 2012, The Transparent Tongue, a massive, inflatable tongue was erected, with bodies extending from the organ and gestating as models passed. The Spaghetti Handjob added large, seafoam ribbons (or "spaghetti"), descended along the runway. The Five O'Clock Leg Alignment was described thus: "deformed yogis are aligned to perform a series of synchronized movements in a controlled rusty red temple." He's incorporated large marionettes, other massive organs and, in a collaboration with Swedish artist Andreas Emenius, a shaggy yellow dragster.

Emenius is a fellow Central Saint Martins graduate. In 2007, they embarked on a series of Fringe Projects—ten pieces "exploring illusion, surface, and movement." The works were completed in performances, videos, installations, and other mediums. The project concluded in 2009, with a book and exhibition at Zeeuws Museum in the Netherlands to follow. The duo then kicked off The Circular Series in 2009. From a statement: "Like in their earlier collaboration The Fringe Projects where the fringe is used formally, the circle is used as a clarifier, or visual glue, linking all the projects to the same universe. As a formal experiment the circle is interesting in relation to material, form, and motion. If you dig a little bit deeper, the Circular Series is about identity and inclusion, and about a person's place in the world, between fantasy, and [being] self-made."

As of the writing of this book, the artist's latest high-profile project is The Great Chain of Sleepers, a show from July 2017. It took inspiration from an incident in which a performer feel asleep onstage during one of the designer's shows. A statement from the show offered this: "When the eyes are closed and the heart beats quickly, the body and mind becomes disengaged from the surroundings and the breathing becomes more shallow. As we give up our bodies to sleep, sudden twitches escape our brains and we go through a chain of sleep stages." What happens in those stages—with too much sleep or not enough—is the engine of this collection. Like all of Vibskov's collections, the lines between what is reality and what comes from our imagination begins to blur. And the designer keeps creating worlds out of that messy place.+

PREVIOUS SPREAD: Henrik Vibskov exhibition from 2014. Photo by Paavo Lehtonen ABOVE: Vibskov's Land of the Black Carrots show. Photo by Michae Hermansen. OPPOSITE: Shot from Vibskov Performance in Middleburg. February 2009.

1ST FOLLOWING SPREAD (LEFT PAGE TOP L-R): From The Last Pier Pandemonium. Photo by Shoji-Fujii, shot from The-Solar-Donkey-Experiment. Photo by Alastair-Philip-Wiper. (BOTTOM) Costumes and stage for War Sum Up. Photo by Alastair-Philip-Wiper. (RIGHT PAGE): Shot from the Fringe Projects: Henrik Vibskov and Andreas Emenius at the Zeeuws Museum.

2ND FOLLOWING SPREAD (L-R): Sculpture from a Vibskow performance, Vibskow designed products. Photo by Frederik Heyman Quinny.

ribbed bodice and exaggerated shoulders that rise like textile spurs; and leggings, which can incorporate transparent panels, spines, spars, shin padding, or space-age racing stripes. (A customized ensemble was seen in The *Hunger Games: Mockingjay* being worn in the sunroom by President Snow's personal stylist.)

Elena Slivnyak wanted to be a designer, even before she knew what it meant.

"In Ukraine, Russia, and many Slavic countries, it's in the blood and nature of the people to dress well. It is instilled in your brain from a young age," says Slivnyak. "[But] we weren't raised with silver spoons in our mouths... we were forced to be creative."

Slivnyak recalls watching the women in her family knitting sweaters and making clothes, and learning from all of them. Aesthetically, Slivnyak's work is more obviously influenced by her early love of science fiction movies—David Lynch's *Dune*, Paul Verhoeven's *RoboCop*, *The Terminator*—movies in which heroes fight for the survival of whole planets, and look amazing doing it—but the strength, the nous, of the work is one hundred percent Ukrainian. Once in San Francisco, Slivnyak discovered designing clothes could also be a vocation, and there was no turning back. She graduated from San Francisco's Academy of Arts University in 2010; only to be met by the Great Recession.

"I was not able to get a job anywhere, not even in a retail store," recalls Slivnyak, "but I thought to myself, why sit on my ass?"

One month after launching IIMUAHII, Slivnyak's work started getting editorial attention. By 2012, her designs had caught the notice of even the N*ew York Times* and the oft-impenetrable *NY Arts Magazine*, as well as *Project Runway*. Slivnyak competed in Season Ten (unsurprisingly, she lost during the baby clothes challenge) and was brought back to design for *Project Runway All Stars* and *Germany's Next Topmodel*. For someone whose subsequent collections have had more in common with the creations of British architect Zaha Hadid than anything you're likely to see on Bravo's runways, the television exposure was probably less boon than distraction.

In her *Space Opera* collection, Slivnyak offers us dazzling white mini-dresses, coats, and pencil skirts suited to the erotic fantasies of extraterrestrial geometers; feather-gray sheath dresses, jackets, and tunics with ribbing details complex enough to compare to the exo-

skeletons of trilobites or the craftsmanship of Samurai armor. There are hats that fan out like lobe coral or drape like Aiurian plant life; needle-incrusted eyeglasses that menace like mechanical sea urchins or Bene Gesserit challenges. And a commanding centerpiece, aptly named the Alien Queen, with huge barnacle-shaped epaulettes and a battle-ready bodice that gives way to draping so intricate, so graceful, so ethereal, it conjures the flight of deep-sea crown jellies.

As an ardent devotee of IIMUAHII, the cyberpunk pinup and transhumanist pop artist Viktoria Modesta was among the first to flaunt the *Alien Queen*; in 2017, she wore another IIMUAHII creation—a highly textured white jacket set with large domed cabochons which lit up like Modesta's high-fashion prosthesis—for a performance at *The Ghost in the Shell* release party during Paris Fashion Week. And, most recently, in her role on *Killjoys*, a space adventure about bounty hunters, on the Syfy Channel.

Designing for film and television for fellow-futurists would seem like the ultimate dream for Slivnyak but, as a committed environmentalist and animal-rights activist, she has a much bigger one: A present in which people own only a handful of garments of the highest quality (with a few pieces of gorgeous, otherworldly, wearable art for special occasions, of course).

"The fashion industry is the world's second biggest polluter, after oil," says Slivnyak. "I think right now, with everything that's going on in the world, we need to get rid of superficial things and start to pay attention to the real issues."

Slivnyak has always made a point of sourcing high-tech, sustainable textiles (cotton, one of the industry's most common materials, is also among the most pesticide-intensive crops on the planet) but curtailing "fast fashion"—the inexpensive, runway-to-retail model—would reduce carbon emissions and erode sweatshop conditions. While IIMUAHII has never done high-volume production, Slivnyak thinks she can do more, and this is what she envisages for her students at the School of Fashion.

"I'm launching another brand heavily focused on sustainability," says Slivnyak. "In the future, I'm looking to help out by recycling [fast] fashion into high-end pieces that have a long shelf life."

It's a life we'll all want to be seen in, one in which heroes fight for the survival of whole planets, and look amazing doing it. ✦

BEA SZENFELD

BY JEFF D. MIN

Bea Szenfeld is an unstoppable force. She's been called a visionary and an icon, celebrated for designs that have left audiences spellbound. Her resume speaks for itself (Stella McCartney, Tommy Hilfiger, Björk, Lady Gaga), but it's her ability to rise above trends that has made her a juggernaut.

Szenfeld's storied career has modest beginnings. As a child she spent formidable years with her grandmother who during WWII was forced to make uniforms for German soldiers. Before she was old enough to ride a bike, Szenfeld was at a sewing machine, cultivating a skillset that would eventually be her greatest form of expression.

It was instinctive for Szenfeld to work with clothes, but she also understood that when something comes naturally it becomes imperative to challenge oneself. When Szenfeld graduated college she began working in the commercial industry, and while it was an obvious step in her career the experience left her uninspired. What was once a dream was now a nightmare.

"I am not bothered so much about trends and other people's view on fashion, and maybe that's why I was not a good commercial designer," says Szenfeld. "I think it's tiresome and boring to constantly chase trends and keep track of what to like or not to like. Obviously it's important to keep an eye on what's happening out there, but I like to have and create my own design rules."

Getting into ready-to-wear collections was a wakeup call. Szenfeld was eager to achieve, but recognizing what she didn't want was just as important. For Szenfeld, capricious branding took her away from what she most loved about fashion: the fun. Fed up with the rigmarole, Szenfeld quickly shifted gears and started thinking outside the box; feverishly experimenting with all the different ideas floating around in her imagination. On one hand she was forced to adhere to a certain standard, and on the other she was breaking every rule in the book. That dichotomy was significant and tilled the soil for some of her most meaningful work.

"As a student, it was actually my teachers who encouraged me to experiment with different materials," says Szenfeld. "And in recent times, it´s my clients who come up with a proposal for cooperation and suggest a material. In both cases, this is very fun and a great challenge for me."

> "I THINK IT'S TIRESOME AND BORING TO CONSTANTLY CHASE TRENDS AND KEEP TRACK OF WHAT TO LIKE OR NOT TO LIKE."

OPPOSITE: Bea Szenfeld. Photo by Carl Thorburg.
ABOVE: From the White Collection. Photos by Joel Rhodin.
FOLLOWING SPREAD (LEFT): Photo by Joel Rhodin.
(RIGHT) From the Sur La Plage *collection. Photo by Bea Szenfeld.*

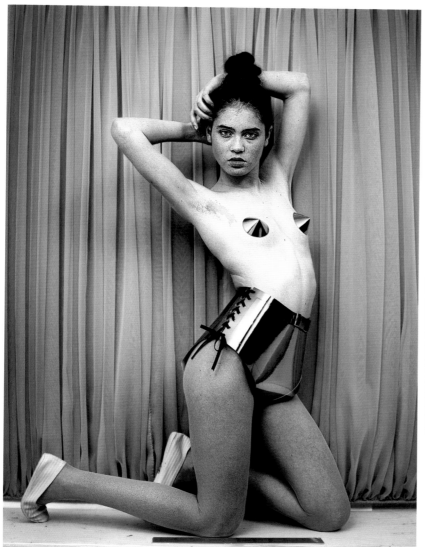

"WE ARE LIKE AN OLD COUPLE... I CANNOT FORCE PAPER TO DO ANYTHING, IT'S A COLLABORATION BETWEEN US TWO."

To truly understand Bea Szenfeld's work it's important to look beyond the aura of greatness and appreciate the humor that serves as her foundation. For example, her bathing suits: one made of Lycra and the other an amalgam of two suits attached at the hip; playfully illogical and against the grain, tantamount to serving Slim Jims and bubblegum at a Michelin star restaurant.

The way Szenfeld combines theories poses distinct challenges; if it's too playful the integrity of the design is compromised, if it's too intellectual the piece loses warmth. To bring harmony to the chaos, Szenfeld relies on unorthodox materials, using everything from pasta, metals and plastic to her most popular weapon of choice: plain old paper. Avoiding archaic standards engages the senses on a different level, and in that awe-inspiring space the virtue of her designs emerge.

"Paper is my material," says Szenfeld. "We are like an old couple, we have struggled for so many years, made it through many fights and tough times. I cannot force paper to do anything, it's a collaboration between us two. Everybody can fold and play around with paper, so for me it´s important to find new ways to work with it. Paper has made me think and create in a totally different way. I think a lot about volume and logistics. It made me look at the human body in a new way."

Haute Papier is a collection of work that exemplifies Szenfeld's feathery touch. Inspired by origami and the Arte Povera movement Szenfeld combined thoughtful Swedish design with silly adolescent hijinks; a meticulously crafted paper gorilla takes center stage hanging on the arm of a stoic supermodel, and what once was distant and out of reach is now accessible to all. It's comical and full of wisecracks, a reminder

to not take things too seriously. It's not a funeral, it's fashion.
Haute Papier was so popular that the Royal Swedish Opera came calling. To bring the campaign to life, Szenfeld teamed up with design powerhouse Stockholm Graphics and photographers Karolina Henke, Carl Thorborg, and Stina Wirsén. The synergy between the collective was electric, and it was an apt way to frame the liveliness of Szenfeld's designs.

"I think there is a very thin line between art garments and garments used for performing arts or on theatrical scenes," says Szenfeld. "It´s very difficult to be a part of both sides. I like to have a high fashion sense and good craftsmanship, and I leave it to others to assort me and my garments. I try to find a balance between art objects and fashion."

Bea Szenfeld is a rebel, but not in the traditional sense. Instead of wielding light sabers

OPPOSITE: From the Sur La Plage *collection. Photo by Bea Szenfeld.*
ABOVE: Photos by Bea Szenfeld.
FOLLOWING SPREAD (L-R): Photo by Bea Szenfeld, Photo by Joel Rhodin.

and kicking over garbage cans she wages war with a cheeky smile and bad puns. Her style is warm and inviting, Christmas in a can. But as welcoming as her perspective is, her congeniality should in no way be mistaken for nativity. Few are as dedicated to their vision and even fewer can execute it with the same level of precision.

In the song "Want Something Done," DC-based lyricist Oddisee pens a story about how hard it is to make it in the rap world—the critics, the networking, the money. The twist is that he condemns those weather-beaten standards, believing that for an artist to succeed all he or she needs to do is listen to their gut, not someone else's. He raps, *Started off locally, and now it's changed globally / That's the way it's 'posed to be / Single seeds only grow to trees if left alone to breathe.* This is Bea Szenfeld's story: an acorn who grew into a mighty oak.

Fashion like many industries of commerce can be black and white. Szenfeld with her blonde hair and buoyant attitude approaches that world with a colorful smile, and through a joyful approach she finds an exhilarating sense of freedom. Longevity is never guaranteed, but for Szenfeld it isn't the fame that drives her but rather preserving that childlike feeling she got when she first sat down in front of a sewing machine all those years ago. Her work is a reminder that it's okay to slow down, take a deep breath and let the imagination run wild.

"The most important thing for me is that the craftsmanship is outstanding and that I try to find new ways to wear fashion," says Szenfeld. "It can be very confusing with all the information the internet feeds us with. Sometimes it's hard to know if my own opinion is really mine or if it is someone else's. Today we are fed with so much information daily, every second. I think it's a good exercise to stop and think about what *You* want, *Your* opinion, why *You* like something."✛

"*TODAY WE ARE FED WITH SO MUCH INFORMATION DAILY, EVERY SECOND. I THINK IT'S A GOOD EXERCISE TO STOP AND THINK ABOUT WHAT YOU WANT, YOUR OPINION, WHY YOU LIKE SOMETHING.*"

PREVIOUS SPREAD: (L-R) Photo by Bea. Szenfeld, Photo by Joel Rhodin.
OPPOSITE: Photo by Joel Rhodin.
ABOVE (L-R): Photo by Bea Szenfeld.
Photo by Joel Rhodin.

NIKOLINE
LIV ANDERSEN

Unless noted, All images from: Only Angels Have
Wings, 2014, Photo by Signe Vilstrup
Make up by Anne Staunsager
Hair by Lasse Pedersen

*ABOVE:
The Dance of the Deaf and Dumb Eye
Exhibition at Horsens Museum of Modern Art and
Designmuseum Danmark, 2011-2012
Photographer Nicky de Silva*

BY CARO

Brilliant, beautiful, and out of this world, Danish fashion designer Nikoline Liv Andersen's work makes a statement that pushes everything to the edge. Through her elaborate works, she channels our dreams and fears, and her most memorable pieces are not meant to be worn. Although her primary craft is clothing, she completely removes herself from the concept of functionality. Instead, the visual component of fashion is the most essential to her, where art lies in the beauty of design and collaboration.

"I call myself a designer because of my education, but I know that I don't work as a traditional fashion designer with collections and fashion fairs," says Andersen. "I just think that to be an artist is such a heavy-loaded term. It is difficult for me to call myself an artist. But I wouldn't mind it if others regarded me as an artist."

In fact, the designer originally thought she might study painting, before pursuing her degree in fashion design at the Danish Design School in 2006.

During that time, Andersen secured an internship at the studio of John Galliano and Christian Dior, whose techniques would go on to influence her approach to making clothes. Traces of their complex and flamboyant designs can be found in Andersen's play of volume and surface. "I loved the fact that everything was made by hand and that the experimental part of the process was evident, even though there always was a tight deadline," she recalls. "It didn't change anything for me—it just confirmed me to continuing my way of working."

Andersen works with unconventional materials to give new life and expression to the clothes. What distinguishes her work from other designers are the many layers of materials and her shaping techiniques that offer surprising textures. Industrial metallic rivets will resemble soft feathers, straws cut in different lengths will have an organic expression, and tedious work of grinding, cutting, and dressing cotton with a sheet transforms ordinary cotton into something fur-like. One of the most complicated garments she ever made was a dress made out of bristly nails.

Every piece is one of a kind and entirely made by hand—a slow and demanding process: "I don't know why I always fall in love with complicated and time-consuming techniques, but I really love sitting there for hours and hours working on things with very delicate details. I have eternal patience when it comes to working with something I believe in...

"I DON'T UNDERSTAND WHY WE ARE PLACED ON EARTH WHEN WE ARE GOING TO DIE ANYWAY. I AM SO SCARED OF DEATH, BUT IT ALSO INSPIRES ME IN MY WORK..."

THIS SPREAD:
"The Dance of the Deaf and Dumb Eye".
Exhibition at Horsens Museum of Modern
Art and Designmuseum Danmark, 2011-2012
Photographer: Nicky de Silva.

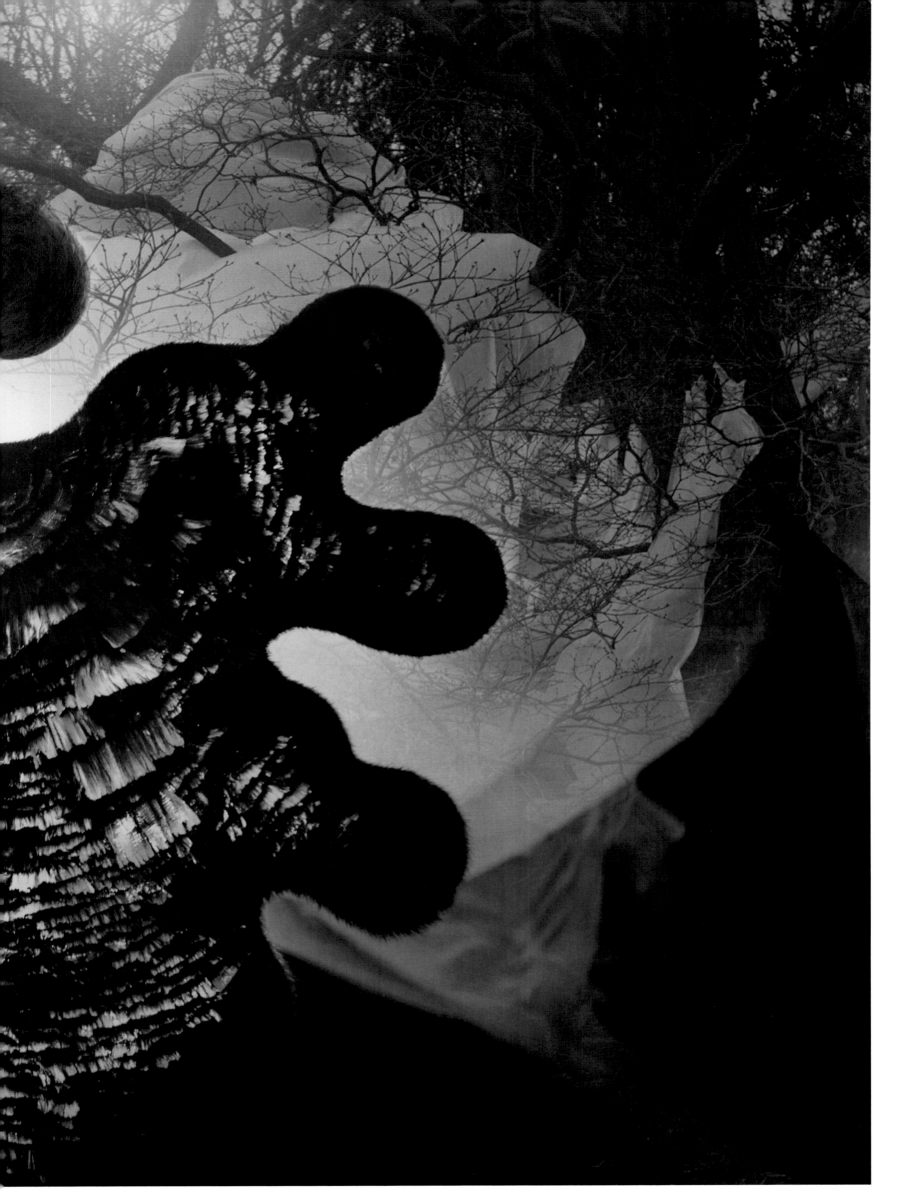

"*I'M ALWAYS SEARCHING FOR A MAGICAL MOMENT... ONCE YOU GET STARTED, YOU CAN'T STOP.*"

I love working with different kind of materials and transforming them. I am trying to create my own kind of artificial nature. My textiles are very detailed often with a system that develops or grows, but without any further details, as for instance, pockets. The silhouettes are often sculptural," she explains.

In her 2014 collection *Only Angels Have Wings* for the Danish Design Center, Andersen's clothing appeared to come alive with futuristic flavor. Each piece employed a variety of interesting materials such as fur, nails, painted mannequins and straws, roughly 45,000 of them. The collection set up an apocalyptic, sci-fi scene: The planet is on the verge of extinction, but humans have developed a revolutionary invention that creates an artificial fabric, giving new meaning to life.

Only Angels Have Wings is exemplary of Andersen's overall theme, investigating the meaning of our existence on this earth. At the heart of her every creation is always a narrative, accompanied by a strong visual concept and artistic installation. "I don't understand why we are placed on earth when we are going to die anyway. I am so scared of death, but it also inspires me in my work," she shares.

As soon as a garment is placed on a model, a character is immediately brought to life. Andersen's models or "androids" live out their fantasies in a bizarre dream world: "For me, a garment comes to life when it is dressed on a body. It can be a real human being for a photo or a performance, but it can also be on a doll for an exhibition. I have been working a lot with mannequins by transforming them, cutting in them, giving them new flexible joints, painting on them and so. I like the fact that they look alike but are not."

The theatrical nature of her work has attracted several famous collaborators that recently includes Icelandic singer and style icon Björk. Andersen made costumes for Björk's *Vulnicura* Tour in 2015 and it was a match made in heaven. Known for her ethereal and innovative music, Björk's choice of fashion on tour was equally dramatic and extraordinary. The intense process behind Björk's costumes involved sewing together small pieces of recycled fur cut out from a classical Saga Furs coat and printed metal foil on top. The result was gorgeous and scary—a reflection of the record's expressionist album artwork.

Today, Andersen keeps a studio in the floor above her Copenhagen home, where she lives with her family and husband, her most frequent collaborator. "Often, it's only me at the studio, but from time to time, there are also interns and in busy times, I have a tailor. And then my husband is often a part of the projects. It's great to share that. My projects are very personal to me and I have my hands on every part of a process," she says. "When I am working with my own projects, I don't really think about certain trends. Actually, I try to forget everything about what other designers are doing."

Andersen may not be influenced by trends, but her offbeat point of view continues to captivate trendsetters in the industry who are seeking to stay fresh and relevant. Last year, she added Fendi to her list of clients when she joined the fashion house as a designer, though their project together remains a "top secret." On what keeps her going, Andersen says, "I'm always searching for a magical moment. It is often a moment in the experimental part of the process where even though I find what I was searching for, I didn't know how to get there when I started. Once you get started, you can't stop."✦

NOA RAVIV

BY CARO

Noa Raviv has always been fascinated with creating her own textiles. The invention of 3-D printing has allowed this New York-based Israeli designer to create new textiles that do not exist anywhere else. Her couture creations have been described as manifesting the aesthetic phenomenon of "hypertexture," simulated surface textures that blend practical clothing with sculptural fantasy.

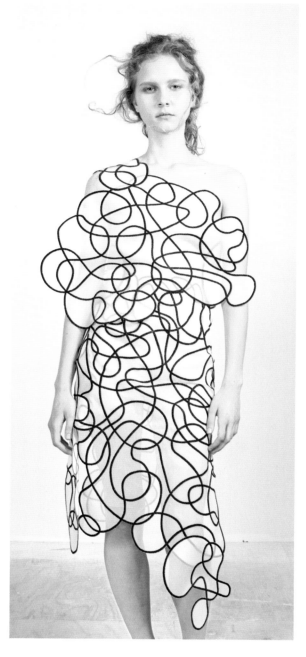

"I was always interested in what other people are wearing and what does it say about them. Clothing is a way of communication that can sometimes be direct and at other times can be very subconscious. Art and fashion are two big loves of mine, and although I was trained in college as a fashion designer, somehow in recent years I find myself drawn much more into art than fashion," she shares.

Raviv first worked with 3-D printing company Stratasys to develop digital models that would serve as the inspiration for her work. Stratasys has been a defining force in 3-D printing and additive manufacturing, shaping the way things are made. She chose the defective 3-D models that her software generated, too structurally unsound to actually print in three dimensions, to inspire her clothing patterns. Interested in the idea of turning something that only exists in the digital realm into a physical object, her designs surpass the limitations of the 3-D printer with the human hand.

"To me there is no hierarchy between the methods; 3-D modeling, drawing, sketching or draping, are all part of my practice," she explains. "When I work, it usually starts with hand work; I love to play and manipulate fabrics, fold, cut and see what the material can do and what can be done to the material. Afterwards, I use the computer and other machine-driven processes, such as laser cutting and 3-D printing, as tools that can expand my possibilities and options as a designer."

For her graduation project at Shenkar College of Engineering and Design in 2014, Raviv debuted her widely acclaimed collection, *Hard Copy*. The collection included seven dresses featuring black and white ruffled fabrics and grid-like patterns that form voluminous shapes. One of its show-stoppers was a stunning black dress that seamlessly incorporated a three dimensionally printed element created on the Objet500 Connex3 Color Multi-material 3-D printer. Dominated by grids that encase organic patterns, Hard Copy articulated humanity's precarious position between nature and technology.

Since then, Raviv has gone from a relatively unknown name in the fashion scene to a relevant up-and-coming designer with an impressive resume. In May 2016, she got her big break when items from her collection were selected by Andrew Bolton, Head Curator of the Metropolitan Museum of Art's Costume Institute, to appear in the "machine-made" side of *Manus x Machina: Fashion in the Age of Technology*. Raviv's contributions to the exhibition were all inspired by technical glitches.

Raviv took this concept one step further for her fall 2017 collection, *Non-Place*, featuring more tech-inspired touches. The term "non-places" was first coined in the 1990s by French Anthropologist Marc Augé to refer to transient spaces that hold no real sense of place or history for people, such as motels, shopping malls, or airports. Today, this also counts the online world, which Raviv describes as a place "where we remain anonymous and lonely."

> "...IT FEELS LIKE THE INTERNET IS EVERYWHERE, BUT IT'S ALSO NOWHERE."

OPPOSITE:
From the Hard Copy Collection. Photo by Ron Kedmi.
ABOVE: From the Off-Line Collection.
Photo by Ryan Duffin.
1ST and 2ND FOLLOWING SPREADS :
Hard Copy Collection. Photos by Ron Kedmi.

"BUT I FEEL LIKE THE SCALE IS CHANGING AND MY RECENT WORKS ARE NOT GARMENTS... THEY ARE MORE SCULPTURES AND INSTALLATIONS..."

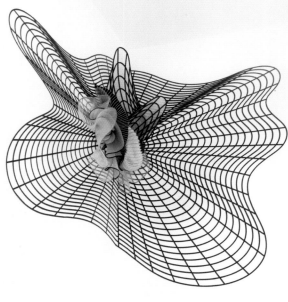

In an interview with *Vogue*, she shared, "I wanted to take that concept in a digital direction, and address how we spend so much time on websites and e-commerce. What are those places? They don't really exist. They're places where we feel anonymous, or even lonely. Our mind is focusing on so many different things, so it feels like the internet is everywhere, but it's also nowhere."

Non-Place has helped to redefine Raviv as more than a 3-D printing-focused designer, which was entirely absent. Some of the most complicated garments in her collection were handmade, offering the illusion of technology's involvement rather than building upon it. Most of the designs feature fluttering, organic shapes that create three-dimensional forms out of sheer tulle layers. The models appeared to float down the runway like jellyfish in a delicate ballet.

With nothing underneath those unique, translucent pieces, Raviv's creations still aren't exactly realistic for everyday wear: "I do see my work more as art than as fashion. I'm much more interested in the concept and the ideas behind the work, than I am in the wear-ability and the com-merce," she says. "I'm actually working now on a few sculptural pieces that are not meant to be worn at all and I see them as sort of alternative bodies—objects that interact with the environment and reflect another way of using material and textiles in space.

For Raviv, what 3-D printing first enabled her to do was all of the things that she never imagined as a designer. The countless shapes and possibilities that the software created remain her inspiration, now serving to inform her future designs. Conceptually, Raviv still works around the same core themes and asks the same questions that she did a few years ago:

"I'm still working around the tension between 2D and 3D, handmade and computer made. But I feel like the scale is changing and my recent works are not garments, but they are more sculptures and installations... For me, it's about using those ideas in other ways, and mixing rich, traditional techniques with technology to create something new that refers to the past." ✦

PREVIOUS SPREAD:
From the Hard Copy Collection. *Photo by Ron Kedmi.*
OPPOSITE: From the Non-Place Collection. Photo by Ryan Duffy.
ABOVE, LEFT: Installation sculpture by Noa Raviv.
ABOVE, RIGHT: From the Non-Place Collection. *Photo by Ryan Duffy.*
OPPOSITE: From the Hard Copy Collection. *Photo by Ron Kedmi.*

ENID
ALMANZA

THIS SPREAD:
"Illumination Editorial"
Photographer: Juan Correa
Model: Joy Stacey
Creative Director: Enid Almanza

PREVIOUS SPREAD:
"The Invention of Emma "
Photographer: Edward Lai
Hair dresser: Dennis Clendennen
Hair stylists and assistants: Brandon Molinet, Alexa Covarrubias, Liz Alfred, Tara Elle, Brittany Meritt, Noemi Gutierrez.
Creative Director: Enid Almanza
Models: Sanya Ismail, Tyler Broussard, Diego Ramos, Britanni Branch, Marcela Rivas, Karina Diallo, Jasmine Beguesse, Amber Ball, Honey Greenwood, Brandon Arvie. Production manager: Evey's Room
Production Assitants: Jessica Mejia, Caro MenjivarMakeup artist: Lila Roberti, Jewelry: Chabahll by Manuela Viana

BY SILKE TUDOR

During one sweltering Texas summer, while living in his parents' garage, Enid Almanza found himself in the throes of heartrending breakup. The on-again-off-again relationship had been long and fraught but now that it was over, Almanza felt that he had no one to talk to.

"I still wasn't comfortable sharing my sexual preference with those around me," says Almanza. "So the only thing that kept me sane during that difficult situation was art."

Almanza dove into his work, sleeping for two or three hours at a stretch, then working, as if in a fever, until he couldn't work anymore. He slept with a notebook under his pillow, curling up with his creations, hanging them above his bed, from the ceiling fan, all around him so they would be the last thing he saw when he closed his eyes and the first thing he saw when he awoke. His dreams were crazy—hypervivid, psycho-sexual, beautiful, sad.

"Extraterrestrial technology and divine mythology, all mixed up," recalls Almanza. "I would get up in the middle of the night and just sketch like a madman."

Almanza cried a lot, sometimes making a garment, only to destroy it when it was done, and remake it once it was in tatters. It felt like madness. He lost weight. His fingers bled. But, in the end, House of Enid was born.

Almanza took photographs of his work, using his sister and cousins as models. The images, often taken near open ocean, were allegorical and primal, and nearly unforgettable, with "models" dressed like archetypes from the greatest unknown sagas in the universe. The photos were chosen for magazine covers and editorials, and whisked around the internet by *Vogue Italia*. By the time Almanza was ready to officially launch his collection, Houston was buzzing. Professional models, make-up artists, and photographers lined up to help. The well-known Redbud Gallery offered to host an exhibition of the work. And *House of Enid: Illumination*, Almanza's first runway show, was standing room only. He was twenty-three.

"That was the night I finally understood what I was meant to do," says Almanza.

Almanza comes from a family of modest means and rich artistic traditions—poets and painters of great talent, including his father, his grandfather, and at least two aunts. He was born in the small but cosmopolitan city of Guanajuato, Mexico, nestled in a valley amidst abandoned silver mines. Once a crown jewel of a colonial empire, Guanajuato boasts lacy balconies that overlook the zocalo, cemeteries that are filled with mummies, soaring churches with twenty-four-karat altars, stairways that stretch into the mountains, and tunnels that run beneath the city like honeycomb.

"I was thirteen years old when we left Mexico," says Almanza. "But, when I returned, ten years later, I immediately noticed the direct influence of

"I WOULD GET UP IN THE MIDDLE OF THE NIGHT AND JUST SKETCH LIKE A MADMAN."

"FOR A GUY WHO WAS DESIGNING OUT OF HIS PARENTS' GARAGE, THAT WAS HUGE"

[the city] on my work—it was a surprise." Invoking the awe of Catholic iconography and the unearthly thrill of a far more ancient royal court, the golden masks, headdresses, and eyeglasses at the center of Almanza''s collection, *Illumination*, are rich with symbolism, psychic power, and perverse possibility. Small, blood-red roses are impaled, like the Madonna's constellation of stars, on a halo of golden spikes that radiate from eyeglasses comprised of baroque filigree; an ornate crown of gold clothespins complements a demonic facemask, which offers, as its only recognizable feature, a yawning, metallic maw; a swarm of powdery, gold-leafed butterflies alights on a hat-shaped trellis; a bondage hood is encrusted with hundreds of small, gilt zipper-pulls and worn above a Dada-esque cape of perforated sheet-metal; bulbous goggles, like the eyes of an alien bumblebees, are trimmed in pearls; sunbursts of aureate forks, feathers, and other common artifacts balance a mini-dress made of industrial tubing sewn in endless coils that resemble clouds from imperial robes.

Here, eyes, the poetic interface to the soul, are completely hidden from view, suggesting that the flesh bodied beneath must channel visions from another source, while each fingernail is augmented by a lethal, jewel-encrusted metal claw.

Almanza doesn't recall being particularly creative as a child but, in a foreshadowing of things to come, he remembers messing with his sister's Barbie dolls—altering their clothes by putting shirts around their legs, covering their faces with fabric or mats of hair which he cut and colored with crayons. He also remembers observing his mother as she meticulously prepared to go out into the world, slipping silver rings onto her long fingers, a ritual which he would later take up as his own and feed into his work. "Growing up in that artistic environment as a child was truly enriching, and magical," says Almanza. "But, it was also a bit intimidating [because] I didn't know if I could ever achieve that same level of excellence... Then we moved to a different country."

In Houston, Texas, where English became his second language, Almanza decided to keep his head down and study computer engineering.

"I just wanted to fit in, to be average, or not be noticed at all."

The tactic was short-lived. Long before the Almanza had completed high school, he'd found the work of Alexander McQueen and, by proximity, a pantheon of similarly-minded creatives, from Thierry Mugler to Nick Knight. Before long, Almanza was using his computer skills to articulate the images in his head. At eighteen, he finally bought some cheap fabric to see what he could achieve. His approach to headdresses and eyeglasses was more organic; he constructed them without drawings, allowing them to emerge like sculpture, from materials he had at hand. Like the glasses—with lenses made from soda-can tops—that he sent to Lady Gaga when he was twenty-one. Within the year, she wore them, on *The Muppets Holiday Spectacular* with Elton John.

OPPOSITE AND ABOVE RIGHT: "Beautiful Decay". Photographer: Cameron Durham. Models: Ndidi Ogah and Karina Diallo. Creative Director: Enid Almanza. Makeup: Eliana Olivo. Production Assitant: Kevin Almanza.

ABOVE, LEFT:
"The Undone And The Divine "
Photographer: Juan Correa. Model: Enid Almanza. Stylist: Melanie Almanza.
PREVIOUS SPREAD, LEFT: "The Invention Of Emma". Photographer: Edward Lai. Hair Dresser: Dennis Clendennen. Hair Stylists And Assistants: Brandon

Molinet, Alexa Covarrubias, Liz Alfred, Tara Elle, Brittany Meritt, Noemi Gutierrez. Creative Director: Enid Almanza. Model: Amber Ball Production Manager: Evey's Room. Production Assitants: Jessica Mejia, Caro Menjivar. Makeup Artist: Lila Roberti. Jewelry: Chabahll By Manuela Viana.

PREVIOUS SPREAD, RIGHT: "Beautiful Decay". Photographer: Cameron Durham. Model: Marcela Rivas. Creative Director: Enid Almanza. Makeup Artist: Eliana Olivo. Production Assitant: Kevin Almanza

"THE FACT THAT A PIECE OF METAL CAN MAKE YOU FEEL MORE POWERFUL, OR MORE BEAUTIFUL, OR GIVE YOU CONFIDENCE, IS SOMETHING THEY DON'T TEACH YOU IN FASHION SCHOOL…"

"For a guy who was designing out of his parents' garage, that was huge," admits Almanza.

When *Illumination* finally emerged from Almanza's emotional crucible, with its elemental forces of water and sunlight, passion and pain, deities and demons, high art and low brow, collectors took notice. They bought pieces, and Almanza was offered scholarship from *Vogue* to study fashion design and visual merchandizing in Milan. Not long after his first runway success, he left for Europe, to begin work on his second collection.

Followers of House of Enid know that Almanza is never seen without eyeglasses or a mask; and his hands habitually drip with rings— huge, ostentatious rings with snapping jaws or enormous stones; smaller rings, up to thirty at a time, which have been gathered in far-flung towns or from further-flung exes. The rings, a self-confessed homage to his mother, are like an identifying crest, or a group of talismans that keeps the world at bay.

"The fact that a piece of metal can make you feel more powerful, or more beautiful, or give you confidence, is something they don't teach you in fashion school," says Almanza.

Since going abroad, Almanza has kept his family close—his sister is House of Enid's makeup Artist; his brother is the Choreographer behind Almanza's award-winning fashion-film directorial debut, his mother provides meticulous embroidery, and his aunts provide sage advice. While Almanza constructed *Illumination* almost single-handedly, he speaks with great warmth about busy days in the studio with his intimate crew, braced by his head seamstress and man-

ager, Evey—the very first person he ever trusted to help him bring a design to reality.

"We always have fun, that is the important thing," says Almanza, "And the music must be loud, very loud. No matter what it is."

Florence and the Machine, iamamiwhoami, The Knife, Guns N' Roses, all of it blaring through the speakers, mannequins everywhere, clothespins flying; people sewing, embroidering, singing, dancing, shouting questions. This is the sweet spot. And, still, even buttressed by loved ones, the act of creation can be frightening. The heart, after all, is a fragile thing.

"More than anything, I'm a story teller," says Almanza. "This is a book that I'm writing and, with each collection, I will write a new chapter."

"With this new collection, I'm completely out of my comfort zone," says Almanza, admitting that he suffered from love, loss, and depression in Europe. "I'm opening myself up to the let the world see what's inside, what's behind the mask, what's behind the glasses… I'm sharing the entire journey I started when I left Houston in 2014."

Unlike *Illumination*, which sought to convey the divinity within humanity, Creation promises to explore its darker side.

"What's left when the light goes out?" poses Almanza.

We may assume a very great deal.✦

ABOVE: "The Undone And The Divine"
Photographer: Juan Correa. Model: Enid Almanza.
Stylist: Melanie Almanza.

PREVIOUS SPREAD, LEFT:
"The Invention Of Emma".
Photographer: Edward Lai. Hairdresser: Dennis
Clendennen. Model: Karina Diallo. Makeup: Lila
Roberti. Jewelry: Chabahll.

PREVIOUS SPREAD, RIGHT AND OPPOSITE:
"Beautiful Decay". Photographer: Cameron
Durham. Models: Ndidi Ogah and Karina Diallo. Cre-
ative Director: Enid Almanza. Makeup: Eliana Olivo.
Production Assitant: Kevin Almanza.

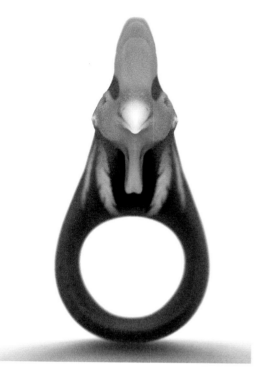

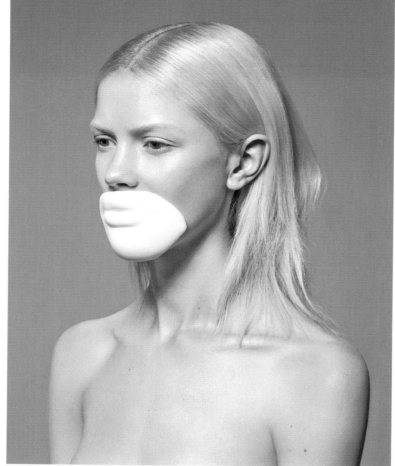

ROB ELFORD

BY JEFF D. MIN

In Isaac Asimov's short story "Satisfaction Guaranteed," the protagonist Claire is subjected to an experiment involving a robot named Tony whose sole purpose is to obey orders and abide by The First Law of Robotics, which is to do no harm to humans.

At first Claire is skeptical. She finds herself on edge, tense and frightened by the robot's human-like characteristics. Over time, however, she warms to Tony; eventually revealing to him some of her deepest, most intimate thoughts. Predictably Claire falls for Tony and they consummate their relationship in a final act of forbidden love.

Asimov's future is here, at least in theory. Society and technology are assimilating at a rapid clip, leaving us to question the parameters of the human experience. Rob Elford, a London-based artist who focuses on sculptural jewelry design asks equally ambitious questions, inquiries that would make Asimov's eyes twinkle in delight.

"My work has a real emphasis on how cultural and political ideologies evolve and distort over time," says Elford. "Particularly how different schools of thought have conflicting ramifications when applied to different endemic cultures."

Elford constructs his narratives around timeless tropes: necklaces, rings, bracelets, etc. His aspirations, however, has him distorting and exaggerating those traditional forms. He strives to create a delicate balance between "complex, gravity-defying structures and functional wearable pieces."

"I am definitely of the opinion, that function follows form," adds Elford. "I do, though, try to make sure everything I create can be worn in some way. I try not to approach a piece as a sculpture that also functions as jewelry or vice versa, instead I try to create a synergy between the two disciplines."

Hoodoo Botanica is a collection of work that explores the relationship between voodoo culture and modern religious ideologies. Unable to visit Haiti for safety reasons, Elford traveled to the U.S. to conduct research; he broke bread with voodoo priestesses, traversed graveyard shrines and witnessed ritual healings take place in *botánicas* (voodoo shops) in Little Haiti, Miami.

"THE COLLECTION BECAME A VISUAL DIARY OF MY JOURNEY AND EXPERIENCES AND IMPORTANTLY REFLECTED THE ECLECTIC SYMBOLISM OF THIS FASCINATING RELIGION."

OPPOSITE: "The Vacanti Man". Photo and Retouching: Danny Baldwin Model: Kevin McAulay.
ABOVE (L-R): "Chicken Ring" by Rob Elford.
Renders by Pook Studios,
"Monolithic Smile". Photo by Jayden Tang.

FOLLOWING SPREAD (L-R):
"A Wonderful Contortion 2016 (Mask and Monocles)", "The Vacanti Man. Photo and Retouching: Danny Baldwin Model: Kevin McAulay.

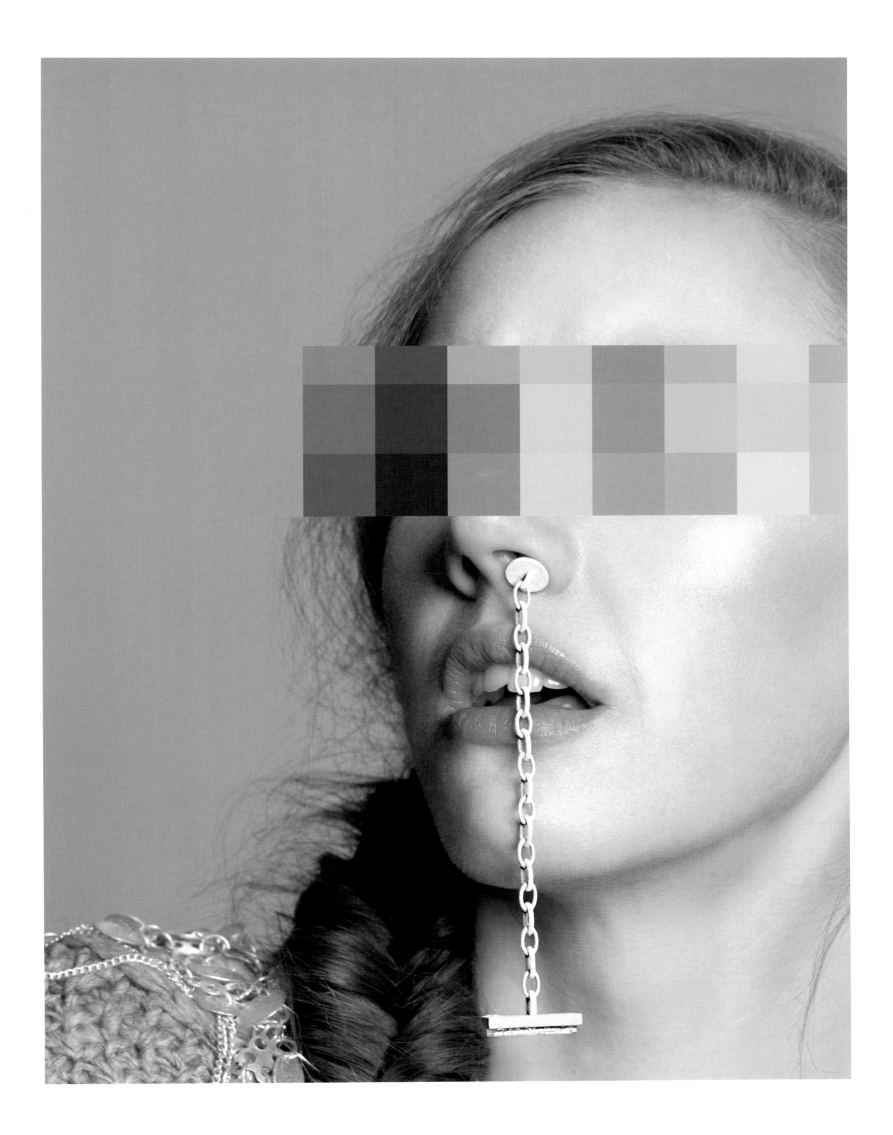

PREVIOUS SPREAD (LEFT):
Jewellery: Rob Elford.
Photo and Retouching: Danny
Baldwin. Model: Kevin Mcaula.
(RIGHT) "Exhaled Glory".
Photo by Roxane Grant.
Hair and Makeup: Erin Kristensen.
Models: Kamila Nowak & Elinor
Krupski.

OPPOSITE:
"White Atlas"
Photo: Roxane Grant & Josh Jones
(Assistant).
Hair and Makeup: Lana Chikhireva,
Models: Sydney Lima & Chris
Machari,
THIS PAGE (CLOCKWISE):
"Love Punch", "Boil the Ocean",
"Icarus Ascends", "Pushing the
Envelope". Renders by Pook Studios.

"*Hoodoo Botanica* was inspired by the Haitian Earthquake in 2010," explains Elford. "I was really troubled by news articles reporting that British charitable aid workers were refusing to aid Haitian survivors unless they converted from their native religion of Voodoo to Christianity. To me this echoed the shameful cultural imperialism of the British Empire, and I felt that this collection could represent a symbolic reparation on my behalf. The collection became a visual diary of my journey and experiences and importantly reflected the eclectic symbolism of this fascinating religion."

For Elford technology is a fundamental tool. His designs involve intricate 3-D modeling, scanning, printing, and hand-finishing. Each piece undergoes a painstaking prototyping process that helps "define viability, wear-ability and [the] aesthetics of each individual piece." As a socially and environmentally conscious creator Elford rarely uses precious stones, instead he opts for synthetic and organic materials like resins, plastics, and ceramics. He is a "technology and innovation evangelist," an advocate who believes that "technologies such as 3-D printing will become a standard manufacturing process in the future."

Vacanti Man is another enigmatic series that encapsulates Elford's ambitions. Inspired by the experiments of Charles Vacanti (a researcher in tissue engineering who is best known for growing ear cartilage on the back of a mouse), Elford utilized 3-D modeling software to turn 3-D scans of arms and hands into low-poly models. The finished product is something out of a Guillermo del Toro film, a fantastical vision that is both alarming and thought-provoking. It's Elford's way of scrutinizing modern society's polarizing view of masculinity; the sports-crazed, beer-inhaling primate and the gun-slinging cowboy with motor oil for blood.

"You only have to look at genuine photographs of men's fashion from the late sixties until the early noughties to see how dramatically our understanding of mainstream masculinity has changed; and as a result, men are experiencing a false nostalgia around our current and much more socially conservative definition of what it is to be male. This is also having a dramatic real-world impact on young men. For example, in the UK steroid use by sixteen- to twenty-four-year-olds, has increased from 0.1 percent to 0.4 percent and more worryingly hate crimes against LGBTQ people have increased by almost eighty percent since 2013."

For Asimov, Tony didn't bring about the end of Claire's humanity; he only exposed what was already there, a woman torn between her heart and mind. Fornicating with a robot left Claire horrified, but what's more terrifying is that she would deny herself the right to her own feelings—intrinsic emotions that add texture to experience.

Elford utilizes technology to visualize this inner-conflict, and how society exasperates the problem through dogmatic expectations. Cultural norms are volatile, mercurial in nature and Elford takes the time to examine the scars that are left behind, a way to heal and stimulate the type of dialogue that might prevent these crises from repeating.✝

"*...OUR UNDERSTANDING OF MAINSTREAM MASCULINITY HAS CHANGED; AND AS A RESULT, MEN ARE EXPERIENCING A FALSE NOSTALGIA...*"

ASYA KOZINA

BY ANDY SMITH

For Asya Kozina, a piece of Whatman paper from a stationery store is the beginning of a wedding dress, an elaborate Victorian wig, or a fantastical, man-sized beast. The Ukraine-born artist works exclusively with paper—cutting it and bending it into works that straddle the line of fashion and decorative art. She works with her husband, Dmitriy Kozin, to craft each piece using only blank pieces of white paper, which they say allows them to "accent form and conceal secondary details."

The first misconception to dispel is that the pair uses digital tools for their creations. In fact, each of these works are created by hand, without exception. These aren't even graphically designed with digital aid. Asya sketches each piece in detail, after a deep historical study. For a wig creation, Dmitriy uses a blank cardboard structural element which serves as a foundation for Asya's elegant strips (or "strands") of hair. Together, they add and subtract, evolving a given piece until it's ready to be worn by a model of any age. No piece could ever be created twice by Kozina.

Perhaps this tactile, old-fashioned approach is why the pair is able to emulate so many cultures: Mongolian,

Baroque, Scythian, Venetian, African— these are all influencers and cultures honored by these pieces. A statement offers insight on the role these play: "A paraphrase of modern appropriation of history as a set of events cleared from insignias of the epochs, but often full of contemporary emotions and value judgements."

And the outpourings of this path all started because viewers of her paper sculptures wanted to touch them to see if they were actually made of paper. In a sense, that's why Kozina decided to make sculptures that one *could* touch. The result could be tied to Avant-Garde fashion, which abandons any sense of practicality and instead pushes forth a progressive, aestheti-

> TOGETHER, THEY ADD AND SUBTRACT, EVOLVING A GIVEN PIECE UNTIL IT'S READY TO BE WORN...

All images and photo courtesy of the artists.

cally driven approach. A blank sheet of paper becomes more than a material: It's a metaphor for the possibilities of Kozina's work, with its decidedly endless pursuits.

Her approach has led to several collaborations. She's created massive paper horses, birds, and butterflies for the Russian lingerie company Wild Orchid. Her work has adorned the covers of fashion magazines, and both style and wedding photographers have recontextualized her work for new audiences. Her long fascination with Mongolian wedding costumes (as well as those from across the world) led to a long, complex meditation on these cultural icons. The result is some of her most elaborate work to date.

Yet, the artist/designer is best known for her wigs. In a recent statement, she explains how the consideration of these pieces' history plays into her approach: "Baroque and Rococo wigs used to be adorned with symbols of luxury, sophistication and the romantic spirit of the time," she says. "They were frequently bedecked with model frigates and intricate still lives composed of exotic fruits, flowers, and even stuffed birds. This historic trend inspired us to link our paper Baroque wigs with the similar symbols of our time. Wishing to be consistent with the initial style of our paper sculptures, we decided to continue the existing series and so chose the items that would match the style of our earlier paper wigs. We knew at once that we wanted to take up the airplane and the skyscraper as the symbols of our time that are both bright and beautiful. Our new series is a combination of old and new luxury, where the skyscraper rises at the top of an ornate hairstyle, and the plane is decorated with flowers and ostrich feathers."

It's the kind of work that feels at once new and ancient, a feat that starts the same way many artists' creations do: an unassuming, blank piece of paper. ✦

"BAROQUE AND ROCOCO WIGS USED TO BE ADORNED WITH SYMBOLS OF LUXURY, SOPHISTICATION AND THE ROMANTIC SPIRIT OF THE TIME."

ABOVE:
Dmitriy and Asya Kozina in their studio,
creating handmade creations from paper.

SYLWANA
ZYBURA

BY JEFF D. MIN

Mohandas Karamchand Gandhi once said that "a convert's enthusiasm for his new religion is greater than that of a person born into it," meaning that a conscious, deliberate transformation is far more powerful than an inherited birthright. History is full of these pathfinders: NFL running back Ricky Williams gave up millions to explore alternative medicine, and in the end reshaped the mainstream media's perception of athletes. John Coltrane went from junky to spiritual guru, and changed the way the world listened to jazz. After the death of his brother Subroc, Daniel Dumile exiled himself only to reemerge years later as the enigmatic lyricist Doom.

For Sylwana Zybura personal growth and change are absolutes. She herself is a convert: a former linguist/political science major turned photographer. The alter ego she operates under, Madame Peripetie is her way of waging war against status quo. A chance to unmute her perspective and give form to the visions in her head.

"It was a desire to create a non-existent persona that dwells in the explosive surreal creation process, escaping the mundane reality," says Zybura when asked about the Madame Peripetie moniker. "It's a form of drag exposing all your hidden visual inclinations, making them audaciously come to life. The meaning of *peripetie* originates in the Greek theatre meaning a sudden and unexpected change of events. Coming from political sciences and linguistics, photography became an unexpected but also an instantaneous tool in the construction of my own hypnagogic microcosm."

Madame Peripetie is a swashbuckler—a sizzling soprano who pierces through the syrupy baritones of predictability. She welcomes her

perfectly imperfect perspective with unabashed pride, and embraces a vision that is dreamy and fluid, wildly abstract yet still within grasp. In shedding her previous identity Zybura has given herself over to the splashy fantasies that have occupied her dreams. Fashion, sculpture and photography are her mediums and each provide a stage for Madame Peripetie to shine.

Dream Sequence is a visual of Madam Peripetie's world; "fragments of paradise" that embrace the surrealist tradition. It is an exploration of her conceptual world and how it relates to Freudian theory, "the unresolved tension between material reality—what actually happened—and psychical reality—what our conscious allows us to believe happened."

To bring this vision to life was difficult. Most of the effects were created using makeup, prosthetics and wigs, and very little photoshopping was involved. Deconstructed garments and botanical compositions add depth and stimulates the senses with a touch

ABOVE: "58W". Created by Sylwana Zybura and Tomas C Toth.
OPPOSITE: "Lookbook for Martina Spetlova SS17". CGI elements by Sam Rolfes.
1ST FOLLOWING SPREAD (L-R): "Dream Sequence / Explosion", "Dream Sequence / Silver Surfer".
2ND FOLLOWING SPREAD (L-R): Jewellery Campaign for Xiyang Tang '17. "Dream Sequence / Burned".

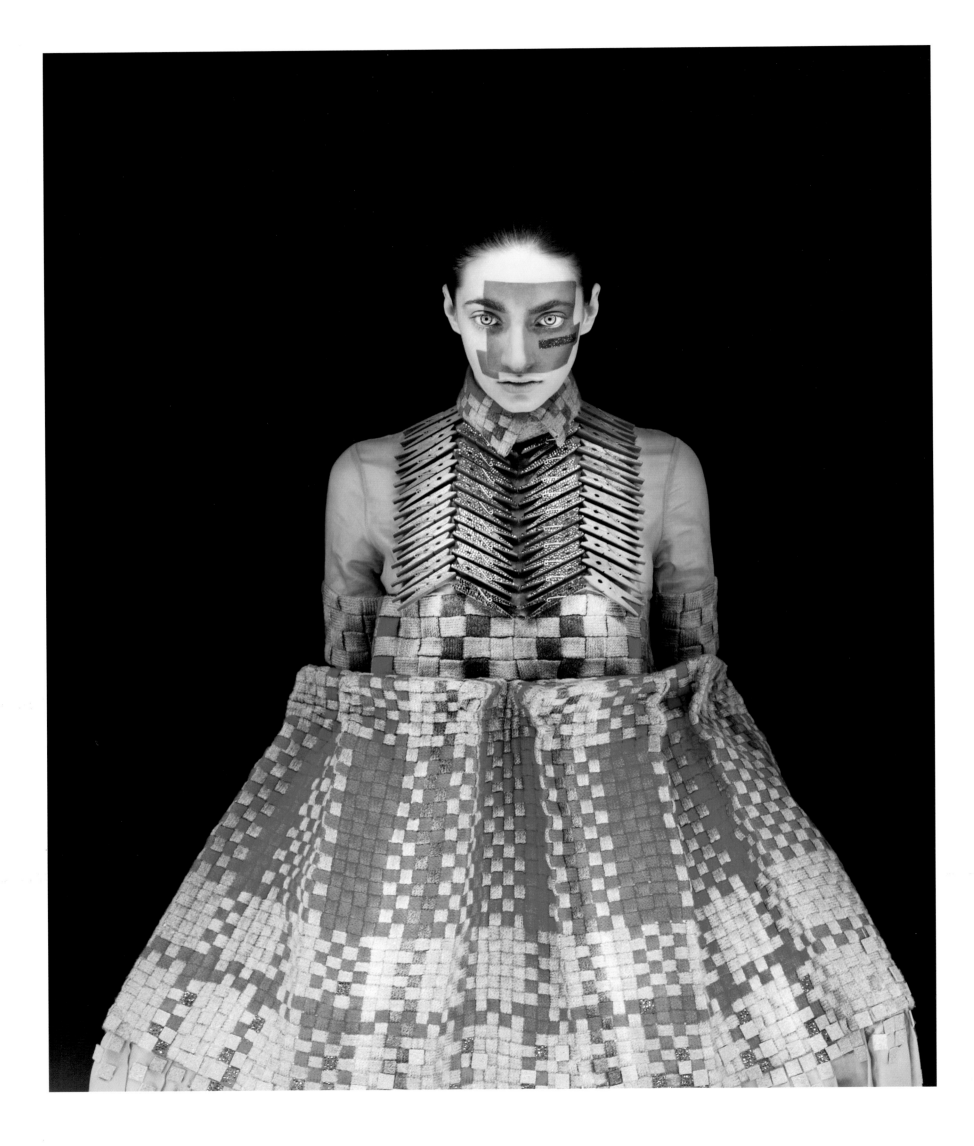

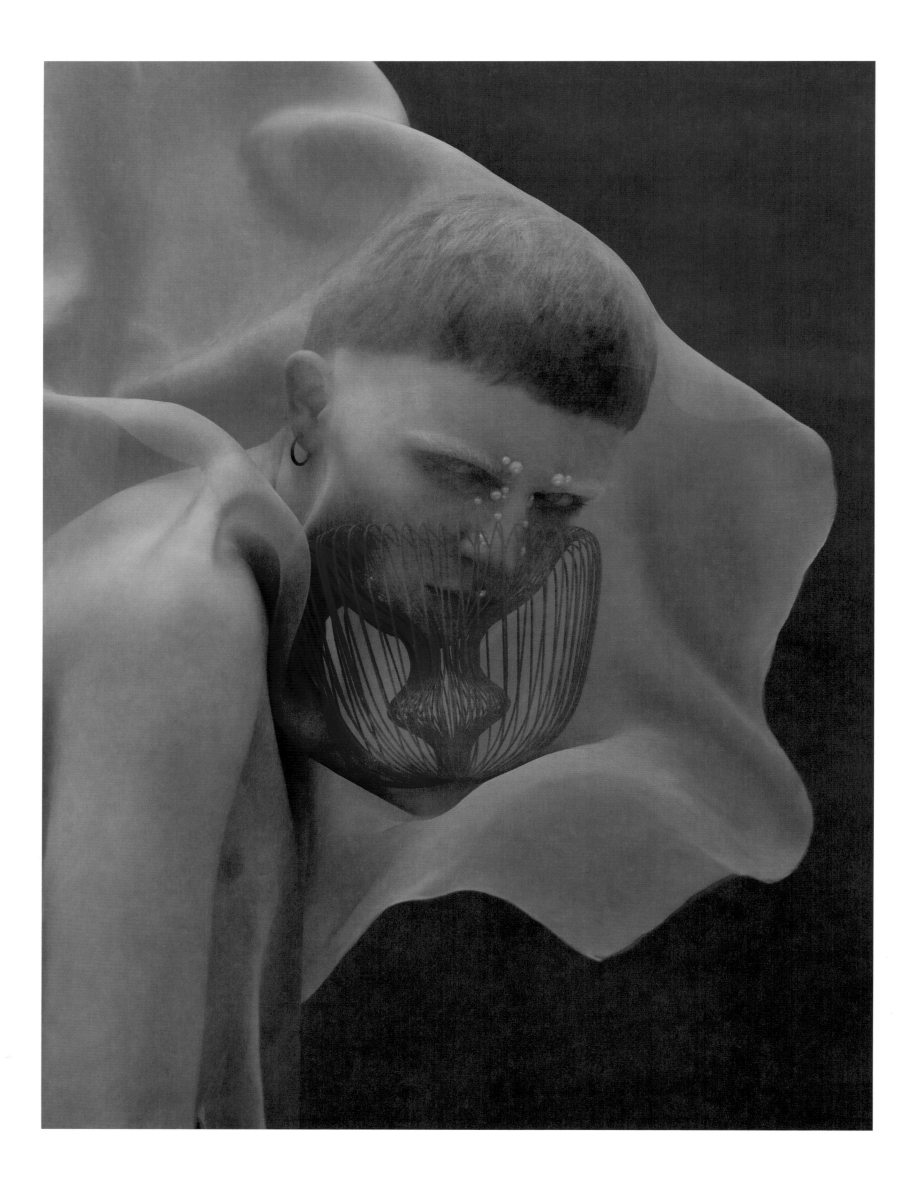

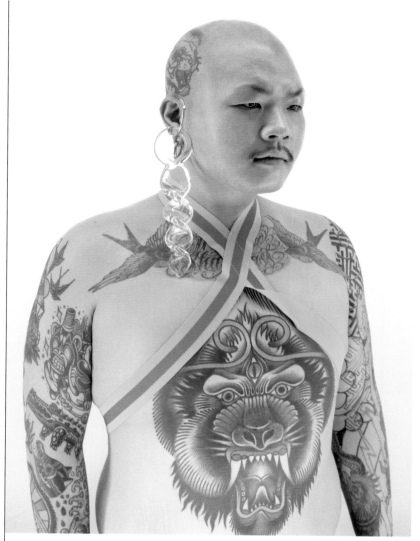

"WE FORGOT HOW TO DREAM AND ACTIVATE OUR TACTILE EMOTIONS; BEING BOMBARDED WITH A PERPETUAL FLUX OF IMAGERY, DESENSITIZING THE WAY WE CONSUME THE VISUALS."

of familiarity. Each character is of its own world, and to truly admire them it is imperative that the viewer set aside their preconceived notions of beauty. They are alien, but close enough to our reality that they might tell us a thing or two about who we are. The characters featured in *Dream Sequence* exist within a chimerical realm where the shores of reality dissolve into the tides of fantasy.

"Dreams are a key component," explains Zybura. "We forgot how to dream and activate our tactile emotions; being bombarded with a perpetual flux of imagery, desensitizing the way we consume the visuals. I love the quote I heard from Nick Knight: 'If you want a reality just stand there.' We need to come back to exploring our desires."

While studying in England, Gandhi made acquaintances with an English gentleman. One evening they went out to the theatre and dinner afterwards. Unfamiliar with the

lay of the land, Gandhi felt painfully out of place. Embarrassed by his lack of polish, he tried to transform himself to suit his new environment; enrolling in elocution classes, dance, and violin. The problem was that his accent was as thick as concrete, he had two left feet, and he was tone deaf. It was a disaster.

Then he had a revelation. He had lived in India his whole life so eliminating his accent was impossible— vain even. And how could dancing and violin make anyone a gentleman? It made no difference. It was all cosmetic. He was pursuing a false idea and in the end decided that he would recommit to what his heart and imagination originally asked him to do, which was stay true to his vision.

Zybura is on a similar journey. She had a choice to make and bet on herself. Madame Peripetie is not an escape from reality per se; she's always been there, lying dormant

waiting for her moment. Zybura is only looking to piece together her ego one daring portrait at a time. The courage she found revealed a voice, and that voice is unfiltered, angular, and exotic—the product of her deepest desires.

When asked what her biggest challenge was when trying to find her creative stride, Zybura responded with, "Making things grow out of your own experience and sensibility. No one can see what you can see." Zybura believes that the individual is powerful and imaginative, but collectively we have forgotten our potential. Our vision has been clouded, and we've been taught that in order to stand out we need to fit in; backwards logic that is muddy and disorientating. Zybura's point of view shows us an alternate path; otherworldly in one sense, but incredibly down to earth in another. ✦

ABOVE (L-R):
Created by Sylwana Zybura and Tomas C. Toth,
"Yourfaceismyfaceisyourface".

OPPOSITE:
Ejing Zang Jewellery Campaign.

PREVIOUS SPREAD (L-R):
"58W". Created by Sylwana Zybura and Tomas C.
Toth, Martina Spetlova Campaign SS17.

DINU BODICIU

BY LIZ OHANESIAN

Dinu Bodiciu's big break came while he was working on his MA in Fashion Design and Textiles at London College of Fashion. Inspired by Jacques Lacan's "mirror stage" theory—the point when children recognize their reflections as themselves—and intrigued by the two-dimensional versions of the self that we see so frequently, Bodiciu designed a collection called *Illusions of Reality/ Reality of Illusions* with the flatness of mirror images in mind. He made hats that looked more like masks. "Whatever we see has to be in front," he explains over a Skype call from his current home base of Singapore. Bodiciu's student show caught the attention of pop star Lady Gaga, who was later photographed wearing the designer's red pantsuit with flattened, pointed shoulders. The attention gave Bodiciu a boost right when he needed it. "It's hard to understand what comes after graduation," he says. The shout-out from Lady Gaga, though, pushed him to continue as a designer.

More recently, Bodiciu further explored how we perceive images, albeit from a different source of influence. With his *Shadowear* collection, Bodiciu created seven looks based on how clothing appears in shadows. Bodiciu took photos of his own shadows as the basis for the designs. Like his first collection, there's a two-dimensional element to the garments, but, like shadows, the elongated shapes morph into unusual shapes with movement. The collection was presented with a performance by dancer Lee Mun Wai and musician Bani Haykal.

"I wanted people to understand that this collection opens up new interpretations of how we perceive fashion, how we perceive garments," says Bodiciu. "This offers a plethora of different ways of wearing them, of playing with them."

While clothing is a part of Bodiciu's artistic practice, hats, which he calls "artifacts," are his forte. "I'm not sure if they can be considered hats, all of them," he says. "Some are in between masks and hats." He makes headwear that sticks to corners of the face and

protrudes into the air, sitting between the spaces of fashion and art. His collections have been inspired by bugs and the human psyche. They meld traditional craftsmanship with modern technology. They are sculptures made of fabrics that can be molded to fit the head.

Before fashion, Bodiciu had studied to be a pharmacist and then earned a degree in graphic design. He spent eight years working with a Romanian theater company called Aualeu before heading to London College of Fashion for his MA. Much of his work, he says, has been inspired by his pharmacy studies. "When we look at ourselves, we only see the skin, but what is beyond that?" he asks rhetorically. Chemistry, biochemistry, psychology, and in particular psychoanalysis, have all fueled his work. "I feel that psychoanalysis is the motor that puts my creativity to function currently and for the past few years," he says.

For each collection, Bodiciu likes to master a technique. It might be laser cutting or 3-D printing or digital printing. He combines those new methods with traditional hat-making techniques. At the time of this interview, he was working on a line that incorporates crochet and macramé. He says "the technicality and the craft" of fashion is part of what keeps him inspired.

In 2013, Bodiciu created the *Specimen* collection inspired by moths and their attraction to light. He made headwear that resembled miters with insect-like iridescent wings and included details like 3-D printed antlers. Bodiciu took further inspiration from powdered wigs, which manifested in soft mask portions of some of the pieces. His couture collection, *Monsters from the Id*, was designed to strip apart the psyche. He used wave-like forms to represent the id. Blank faces stood in for ego to show, as Bodiciu explains in a follow-up email, "the layer which develops as an interaction between the id and alter ego." Faces with features represented the alter ego, "as we are shaped under the influence of the society." He also used laser cutting techniques to represent the connection between the id and how one relates to the world.

Bodiciu drew inspiration from the science of the universe for his *Space/Time* collection. "I had the idea that if I slice a hat and I generate that shape, which is there, but is actually made of very thin layers of fabric, the volume that we perceive is three dimensional, but is made by 2-D slices," he says. In that way, the shape of the hat can be perceived differently depending on the angle from which it is viewed. He calls this "a very primitive kind of expression" of the space-time continuum.

Even Bodiciu's commercial pieces are driven by art. For the past few years, he has been producing a line of baseball caps. Technically, explains, they only look like baseball caps. "It's like a *trompe l'oeil* in a certain extent, but not really that," he says. Where a baseball cap is stitched and uses reinforcement on the brim, Bodiciu molds the fabric. He also adds acrylic bands on the front of the caps. He started making the baseball caps to have something available for day-to-day wear, but it's proven to be creative endeavor as well. He says, "I find that this is an interesting challenge for a designer, to be able to reinterpret an object that became very mainstream, but still give it an understanding of that object and improving the object."✦

PREVIOUS SPREAD (LEFT): Head-piece, photography and concept: Dinu Bodiciu. Model and Make-up: Becca D'Bus. (RIGHT) Illusions of Reality / Reality of Illusions. Photo by Christopher Agius Burke.
OPPOSITE: Head-piece, photography and concept: Dinu Bodiciu. Model and Makeup: Becca D'Bus.
LEFT: "Specimen". Photo by Alexandra Boanta.

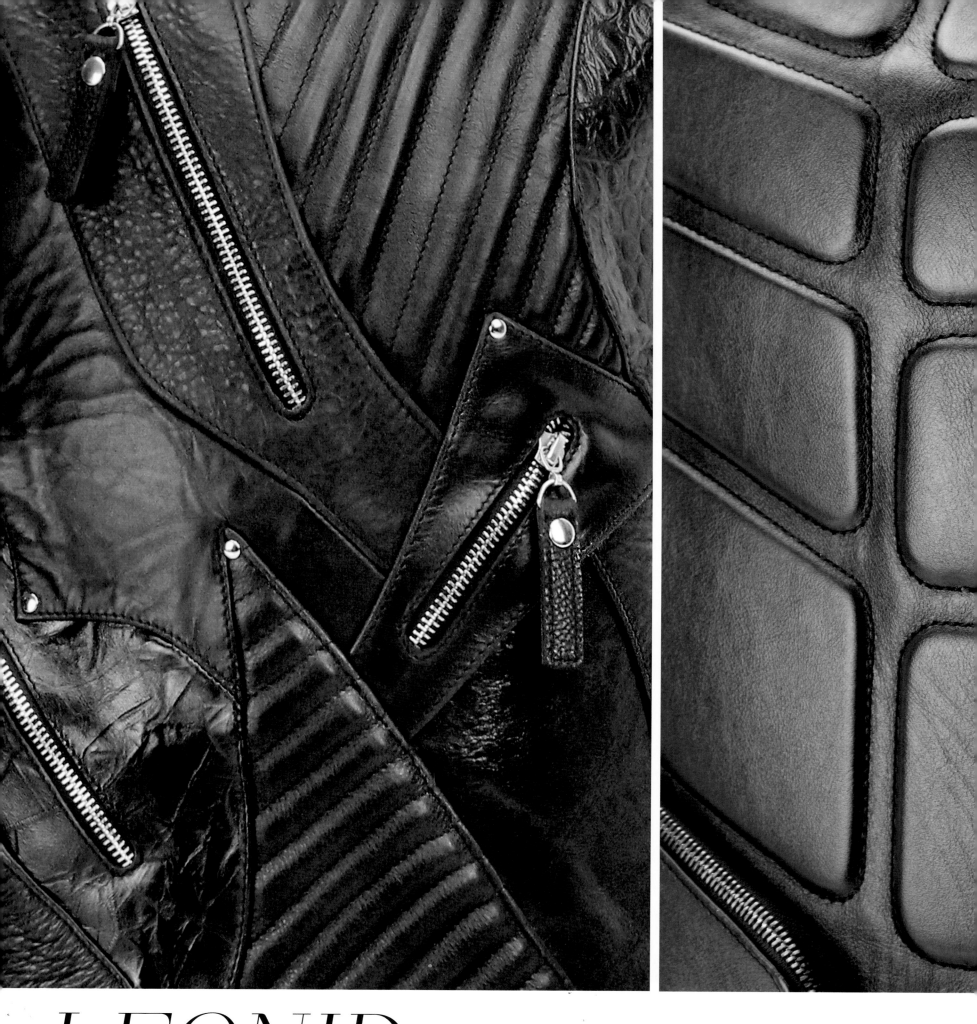

LEONID
TITOW

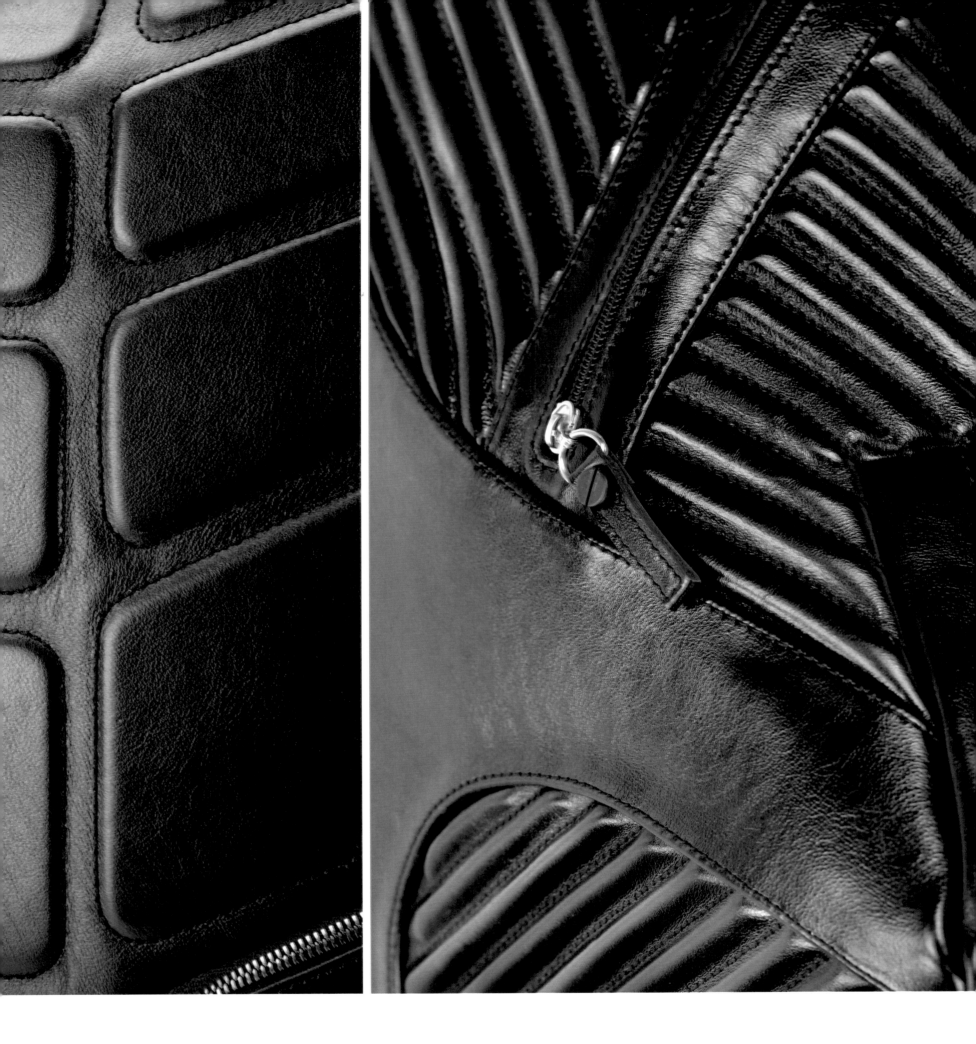

BY LIZ OHANESIAN

In Leonid Titow's hands, even a backpack is art. Take, for example, the Russian designer's "backpack backbone," a utilitarian piece of minimalist sculpture. Crafted from black leather, the visible surface of the "backpack backbone" puffs and indents to give the appearance of a skeletal back. Markings down the center are reminiscent of the spine with ribcage and hip bone-like quilts and pockets on either side. Meanwhile, with his "mosaic" backpacks, Titow uses patches of leather to give a modern spin to a traditional form of art.

Based in St. Petersburg, Titow works frequently with leather, transforming the material into pieces that are functional and sure to make a statement. In email responses translated by his representative, Titow explains that, about a decade ago, he fell in love with leatherwork. The designer appreciated the feel of the material, as well as its usefulness and versatility—adding that he can translate nearly all ideas into leather pieces and can anticipate the results of the project. With leather, Titow has created fashion and accessories that speak to the world we inhabit and the fantastic ones that live in our imaginations.

In his responses, Titow notes that he has difficulty creating capsule collections, although he has plenty of ideas. Instead, he tends to work on one item at a time, likening this to how an artist might approach a painting. His pieces are made by hand, bringing together the expert craftsmanship of an artisan with the vision of an artist.

Titow's bags are amongst his most sedate pieces. Even with these items that can travel easily through any part of society, Titow shows the eye of an artist. A black leather clutch has room to stick your hand between the bag and the rivet-studded strap fixed to the front of it. It's made for an elegant warrior. His backpacks sometimes come in unusual shapes, becoming functional attention-grabbers. Meanwhile, his smaller accessories, like wristbands, point to a punk influence that peppers his overall aesthetic.

Titow's style is provocative, yet polished. It's as cutting edge as anything you'll find inside the nightclub and art districts of major cities, yet there's an elegance to his works. Even the rivets and metal spikes dotting his pieces are thoughtfully executed.

All photos by Maxim Gizatullin. Makeup artist: Svetlana Malaya.

...MARKINGS DOWN THE CENTER ARE REMINISCENT OF THE SPINE WITH RIBCAGE AND HIP BONE-LIKE QUILTS AND POCKETS ON EITHER SIDE.

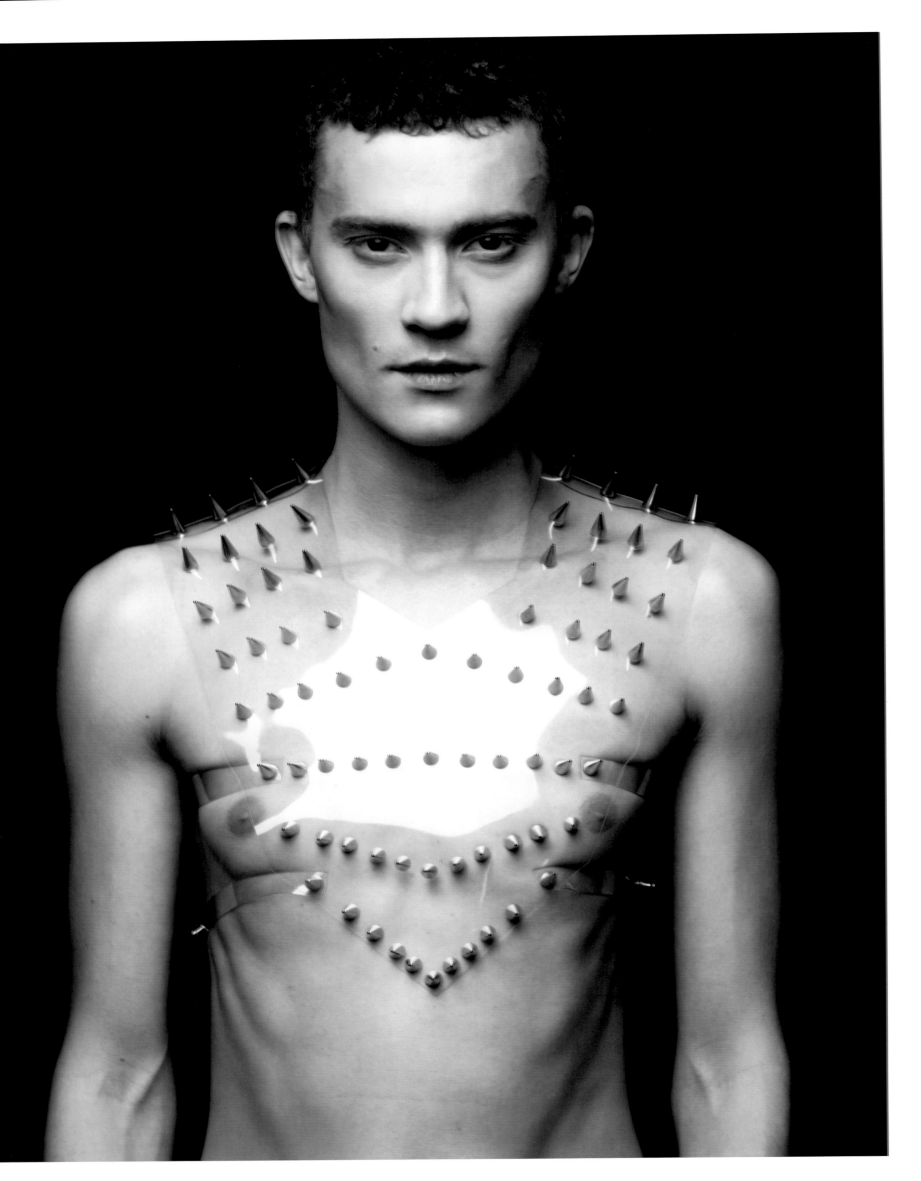

Amongst Titow's more unusual designs are his masks, which have developed over time. In 2011 these pieces resembled fetish gear, but took that imagery into terrain that's more art than kink. One full black mask could make the wearer look like a cyber-pharaoh with its shiny strips framing the face while a large metallic piece with lines cut through the center lays over the eyes as glasses would. Other masks give a far more menacing impression, with spikes protruding from the top of the head and around the mouth while bars across the eyes recall images of prison cells. Even a partial mask—covering mostly the area from the forehead to the nose and leaving the eyes open—is an intimidating piece with its spikes and studs.

In later years, Titow's masks took other forms. At times, they could appear like pieces of armor for the knights of the future, coverings for the face that could protect as well as they might destroy anyone who dared to touch. Some masks could give the wearer the façade of a gleaming silver robot. Others look like the respirator masks of a chic, dystopian world.

In 2013, Titow revealed pieces that made humans look as though they could fly. A jacket's puffed sleeves were downright angelic, while a cape boasted reflective silver pieces that could photograph like the feathers of a creature that must exist only in Titow's imagination.   Titow's garments transform not just the way we see fashion, but how we see the body. His clothes reveal, hide and reshape figures in ways that turn the human form into part of the art. He cuts stunning, cage like designs into tops and dresses, allowing skin to fill blank space and become part of the pattern. He molds shoulders and backs into bumps and lumps, redefining what might be considered a beautiful human body.

His is clothing that creates characters for stories that sit somewhere between fantasy and science fiction, where the mythology of the past meets an imagined future. Titow's designs might show influences from global subcultures like punk and fetish, but they become something else through his eyes. They become the costumes of creatures that inspire both awe and fear, of machines that seem almost human and of the heroes and villains that star in the stories that fill our heads. ✝

KANSAI
YAMAMOTO

BY CARO

Kansai Yamamoto is one of the leaders of Japanese contemporary fashion and gained worldwide fame after taking his designs outside of his home country and later, dressing legendary music star David Bowie in looks that would become synonymous with his stage presence and style. Yamamoto turned his fashion shows into over-the-top spectacles and made intricate costumes inspired by classic *kimonos* and *samurai* pants.

Fashion today is a commercial concept, but in contrast, Yamamoto puts all his time and energy into creating a place where he can get in touch with people's souls. He is not an artist who wants to live unnoticed—never dark and dull, outrageous color and brightness is key to Yamamoto's work. He allies his clothing to the Japanese concept of *basara*, a love of color and flamboyance.

Yamamoto's colorful designs are heavily influenced by classic *manga* illustrations, traditional *Kabuki* theater costume and the Azuchi-Momoyama period of Japanese art, a brief, opulent era between the mid-sixteenth and early-seventeenth centuries. Called *basara*, the art of that period was lavish, decorative, bold and even aggressive. Yamamoto first saw *basara* in traditional, woodblock prints.

"I can feel vigorous energies from its colors," he says. "In *basara*, there are always three fundamental colors; red, black, and white, and those three colors are the most important colors for me as well. I believe that primary bright colors have energy. In addition, pattern from Japanese traditional *Noh* is significant essence in my use of colors."

His career as a designer really took off in the early 1970s, but Yamamoto wasn't always interested in fashion. Before graduating from the Bunka Fashion College in 1967, Yamamoto studied English and civil engineering at Nippon University in Tokyo. Among the designers with whom he apprenticed are Hisashi Hosono and Junko Koshino, Japan's most highly acclaimed fashion designers. He would later collaborate with Junko Koshino to renew the Japanese kimono, reviving interest in this classical fashion.

ABOVE: Kansai Yamamoto and David Bowie.
FOLLOWING SPREAD: Photographs by Clive Arrowsmith.
OPPOSITE: David Bowie © photo by Sukita.

> *" I AM ALWAYS ATTRACTED TO WORK WITH PEOPLE WITH STRONG PERSONALITIES, AND BOWIE HAD AN EXTREME PERSONALITY."*

"To start my carrier in fashion, I had studied designs and sewing under Junko Koshino," Yamamoto recalls. "When I was making clothing from colorful blanket material, she said to me, 'I've never seen such a unique choice of colors like you before.' Her words strike me as pointing out the importance of bright, primary color as the DNA of my palette, even as a young designer."

In Japan at that time, Yamamoto had a hard time finding an audience for his extravagant and extraordinary work. He traveled abroad to the U.K., where he discovered a youth culture that valued a freedom of style, color, and self-expression. By 1971, he was the first Japanese designer to show in London and eventually showed in Paris in 1975.

Among Yamamoto's most famous looks for his costume work with music icon David Bowie were those worn by the singer during his *Ziggy Stardust* and *Aladdin Sane* tours, including wildly printed *kimonos* and space-age-inspired jumpsuits. One of his most memorable pieces is Bowie's billowing, striped body suit, based on a traditional Japanese workman's costume.

The two eventually became very close friends. Yamamoto remarks, "I know I have a very strong personality and I am always attracted to work with people with strong personalities, and Bowie had an extreme personality." At the same time he was working with David Bowie as his costume designer, the Vietnam War was creating deep political divisions and social protest. Opposition with the war led to new, radically different clothing styles.

"The war had some influences to artists all over the world to create what was different from things they had done before the war. In such an era, music, fashion and art had intimate relationships, and me and Bowie were not the exceptions. We didn't distinguish fashion from art at all. It's fashion when worn, and it's art when displayed—that's it," Yamamoto says.

In the '90s, the designer began staging what he called "Super Shows," which combine fashion with music, dance and entertainment on a large scale. These shows aim to unite performers with an audience of thousands and have taken place in locations as varied as Red Square in Moscow, Nehru Stadium in New Delhi, and Tokyo Dome over the last twenty years.

Yamamoto considers the Moscow Super Show of 1993 his most important, the show that launched him as one of the original imaginative showmen of fashion. "I was inspired by the vigor and energy of the people in Russia, where socialism had just disintegrated. There, I came up with an idea to have an event that introduces Japanese culture at Red Square, the center of Moscow," he shares.

"With two years of preparation, I had made the show more than just a fashion show. By that time, I had been working years and years on many fashion events in London and Paris, which made me exhausted and tired by various restrictions and limitations of fashion shows. I had come to think that my lifetime was too precious to do such things, and I had to do things which I enjoy myself."

Within the past year, Yamamoto experienced a "revival" in his work when he was tapped by Louis Vuitton director Nicolas Ghesquière. Yamamoto's signature style can be seen in the prints and mask motifs of their 2018 Cruise collection, followed by the Kansai Yamamoto x Louis Vuitton popup shop opening in Japan.

"Ghesquière got in touch with me after he saw the David Bowie exhibition in Paris," Yamamoto shares. "On the first floor of the pop-up shop, there is a huge *Daruma* moving to sounds of *taiko* drums. The installation is a fusion of my original point of view and the modern style of Louis Vuitton." The collection features designs inspired by Japanese culture, traditional Japanese motifs such as *Kabuki* and *Daruma*, a Japanese traditional doll modeled after Bodhidharma, the founder of the Zen.

Yamamoto is now looking ahead to produce his super show, *The JAPAN GENKI (Energize Japan)* Project in Tokyo in 2018. The project is a special fashion event to show off his latest clothes and send a message of encouragement to post-3/11 tsunami Japan and energize it as it gets ready to host the 2020 Olympic Games.

The spectacle by Yamamoto will be performed all over the world and marks a venture much bigger than fashion: "Now, I am doing only what I love or want to do, compared to times when I was young. However, I am not sure what kind of things I will be interested in. I am getting inspiration from every single thing I come across."✦

PETER POPPS

BY ANDY SMITH

Consider that oft-cited quote by fashion journalist Diane Vreeland: "Give 'em what they never knew they wanted." Designer Peter Popps points to these words when offering insight about his work. "These words have always been my method of designing and realizing ideas throughout my life," Popps tells us.

Popps spent decades in the commercial shoe industry, designing for some of the world's top brands, before striking out on his own in a solo practice that takes his progressive approach even further into a blend of fashion and sculpture. "That was not much of a transition as it's my destiny to exist somewhere between fantasy and reality at all times," he says. "When I design commercial shoes my ideas are starting at the impossible in the present, and to find grip I try to find a combination with reality and the desire or need from the customers."

That fantasy seems to be rooted in the future—or at least, a fantastical version of it. In particular, the work of Popps carries themes of "Avant-Gardism, '60s space-age design, sci-fi, and transportation by magnets," he says. His long fascination with these topics fueled his move to take a more sculpture-influenced approached to shoes. Each looks past our present notions of practicality. "This is how I think, what I feel, and who I am," he says. "I adore innovations and developments from the past, contemporary, and future. In all kind of ways we should watch, feel, and learn from that."

This takes literal form in shoes like the "The CUBiC," a pointed, sleek product made from leather and polyurethane. "The SPHERE," with its circular, smooth appearance, takes influence from another Vreeland quote, "Unshined shoes are the end of civilization." "The LACE-UP CiRCLE" adds studs into the mix, with a specific influence by magnet transportation and, adding another layer of intrigue, bondage. The sum of these shoes is a look toward the future that's grounded in retro sensibilities. Like "The SPHERE," it's a circular mentality that drives these innovations. "The very first mobile phone we saw on television in the series *Star Trek* and the first magnetic public transport technology finds its origin in the early 1900s," Popps shares. "It takes many years to develop these kind of innovations, but look where the mobile phones are today. Also, the Maglev transport technology became reality; and the one in Japan goes over 375 mph. We have seen many flying cars in movies or even prototypes, but when I saw the one at the American cartoon *The Jetsons*, I started to dream from that as a little kid."

OPPOSITE: "The CUBiC". Photo by Tom ten Seldam.
ABOVE, LEFT: "The SPHERE. Photo by Tom ten Seldam.
ABOVE, RIGHT: "The CiRCLE" shoe and "OVAL" neckless Inspired by Avant-Gardism, '60s.
space-age design, and transportation by magnets. "OVAL" is a collabortaion with Jos Kwakkel.
Photo by Armando Branco. Graphic art by Pedro Neves. Model: Sipporo Jack.

"WHY WOULDN'T TRANSPORTATION— OR SIMPLY DANCING—BE POSSIBLE WITH SHOES IN A WAY YOU HAVE NEVER DREAMED OF?"

The forward-thinking designers of the 1960s are also eternal influences for Popps: André Courrèges, Paco Rabanne, and Pierre Cardin all added to the Space Age movement. He also admires Vivienne Westwood's punk sensibilities, Ann Demeulemeester's avant-garde work, and fellow Dutch designer Iris van Herpen. Alexander McQueen is ever-present, while today's younger talent also inspires Popps and his pursuits.

Yet, one may be surprised that a primary influence for Popps is his mother. He has even cited her as his muse. He recalls her proudly showing her dress and high heels ensembles—a deeply affecting confidence. That elegance and self-assuredness is something Popps sees much strength in and looks to in the shoes he makes today. As he told Le Report: "There is nothing more satisfying than a confident woman in

beautiful heels who uses the street as her daily catwalk." This focus on the femininity of shoes takes a fascinating turn with pieces like "The BOW," which comments on the "animality of man" by giving the wearer an "armor shell and the elegance of jewelry for one of the most sensitive spots, which is only available for the chosen one." Here, bondage is again an influence, yet adding even more strength to the female wearer.

In recent years, even the most uncommon designs from Popps are able to be paired with progressive outfit designers. Leonard Wong's "Cell Segregation" mutates fashion to a wilder degree when paired the "The SPHERE." Likewise, a sci-influenced soldier ensemble designed and worn by Sachiko Yusura Fukai is even deadlier with "The BOW." The monochromatic nature of these designs makes them a striking addition—

and in many cases, a focal point—for fashion from every corner of the world.

Yet, with all of his collaborations and successes in art and fashion, Popps is always working and looking to the next line. When new shoes are making their debut, he's already deep into another collection. More than a year can be spent on new lines, and with that, he feels the need to not be "too nostalgic." Popps maintains that we should learn from the past "but not hold onto it." His decades in the business continue to add complexity to that same question: What could we be wearing in the future? Now, Popps adds to this question: "Why wouldn't transportation—or simply dancing—be possible with shoes in a way you have never dreamed of?"✦

ABOVE: Couture: "Cell Segregation" by Leonard Wong. Shoes: "The SWiNG" by Peter Popps. Photo by Sohei Yanaoka. Model: Charlie Melchiori.

OPPOSITE: "The RiNG", by Peter Popps. Model: Djinti Sullivan. Photo by Helene Jaspers. Hair and makeup by Mike Nunes. Styling and outfit: Jos Kwakkel and Peter Popps.

1ST FOLLOWING SPREAD (L-R): "The BOW". Photo and Makeup by Helene Jaspers. Model and Outfit: Sachiko Yusura Fukai, "The SWiNG". Photo by Tom ten Seldam.

2ND FOLLOWING SPREAD (L-R): "The CiRCLE". Photo by Tom ten Seldam, "The SWiNG", Photo by Tom ten Seldam, "The BOW". Photo by Tom ten Seldam.

3RD FOLLOWING SPREAD (LEFT): "LACE-UP CIRCLE". Photo by Tom ten Seldam. (RIGHT): Couture: "Cell Segregation" by Leonard Wong. Shoes: "The SPHERE" by Peter Popps. Photo by Sohei Yanaoka. Model: Charlie Melchiori.

4TH FOLLOWING SPREAD (L): "The RiNG". Photo by Tom ten Seldam (R): Couture: "Cell Segregation" by Leonard Wong. Shoes: "The CONE" by Peter Popps. Photo by Sohei Yanaoka. Model: Charlie Melchiori.

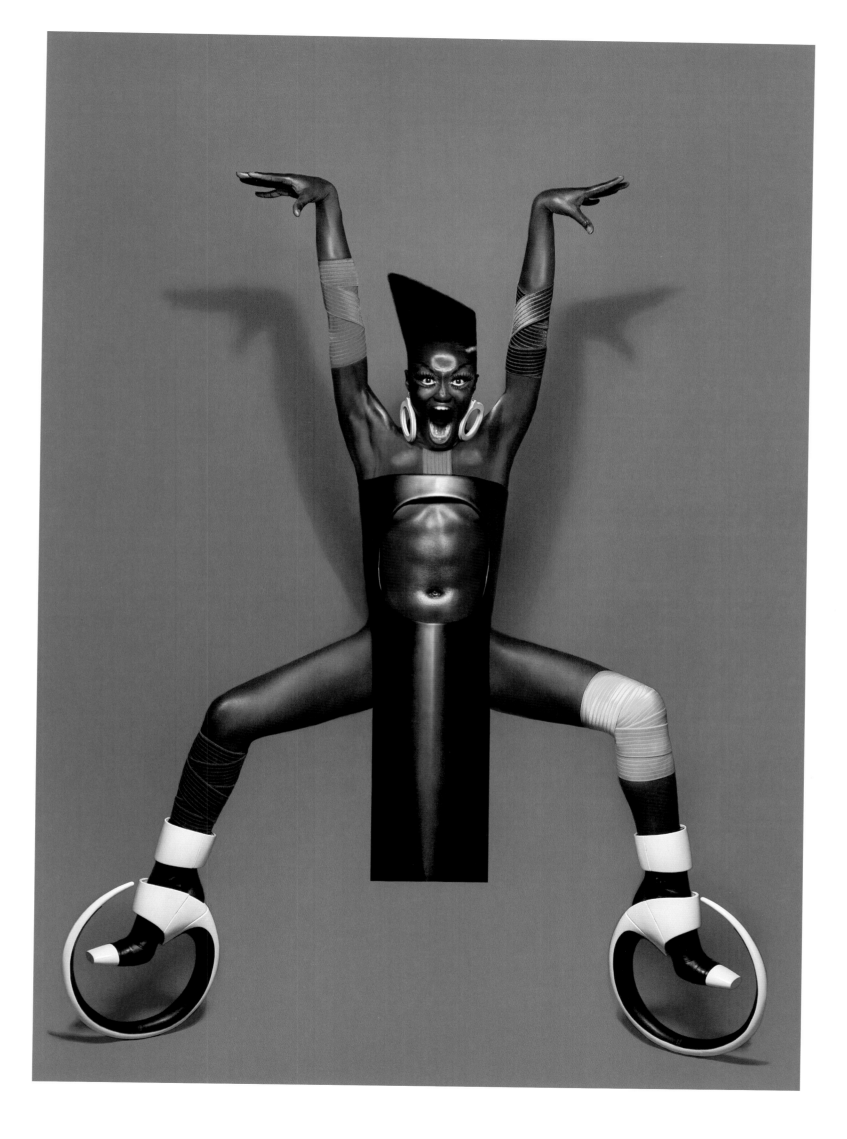

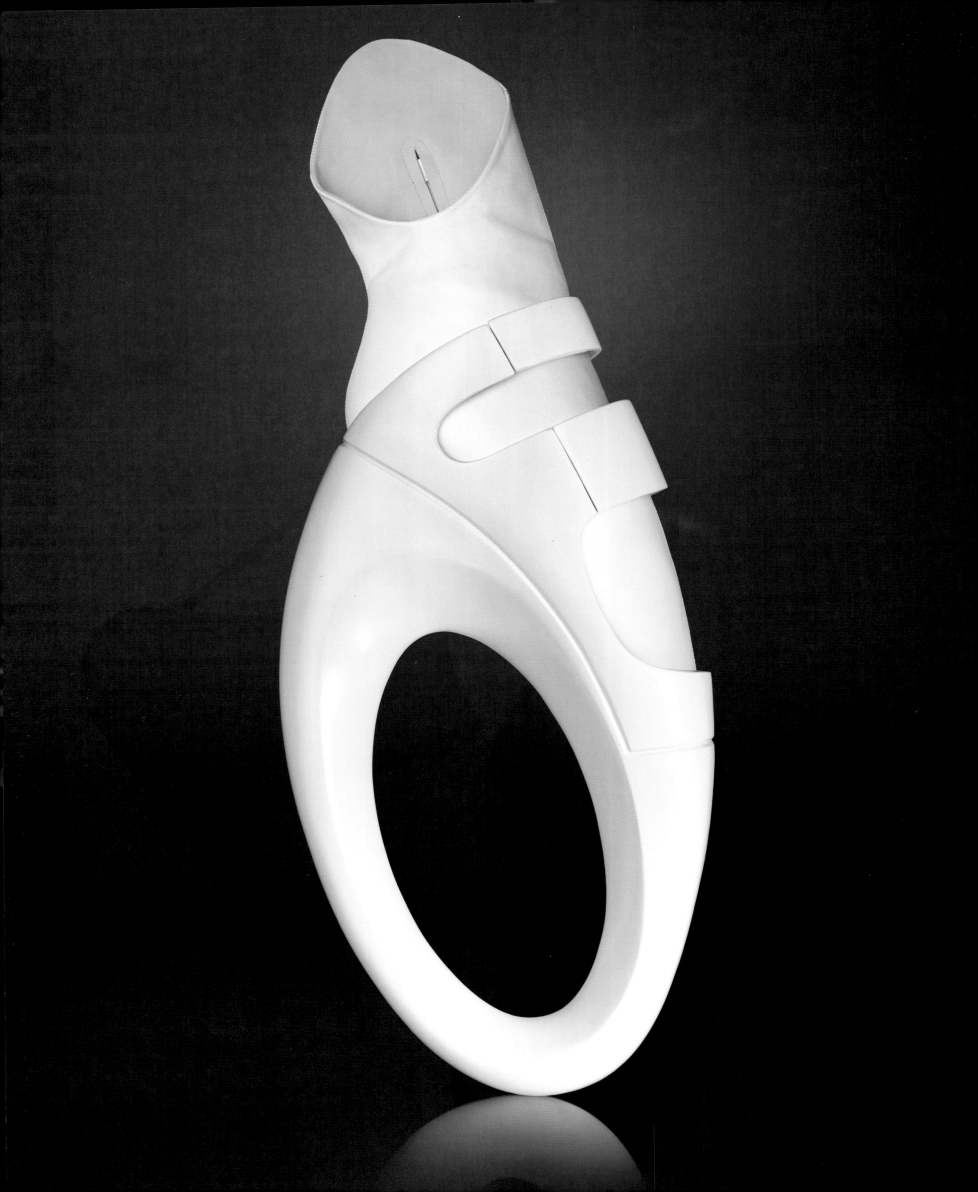

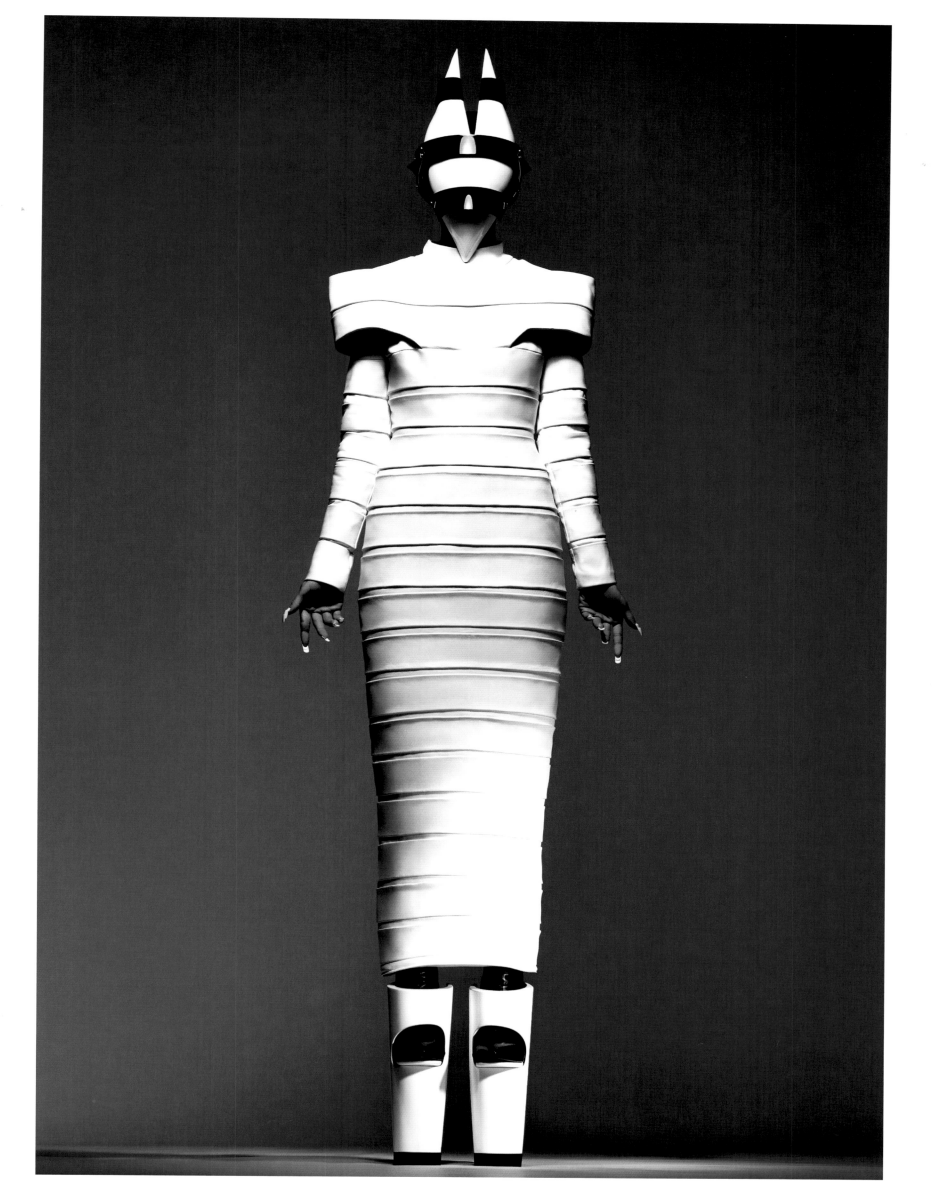

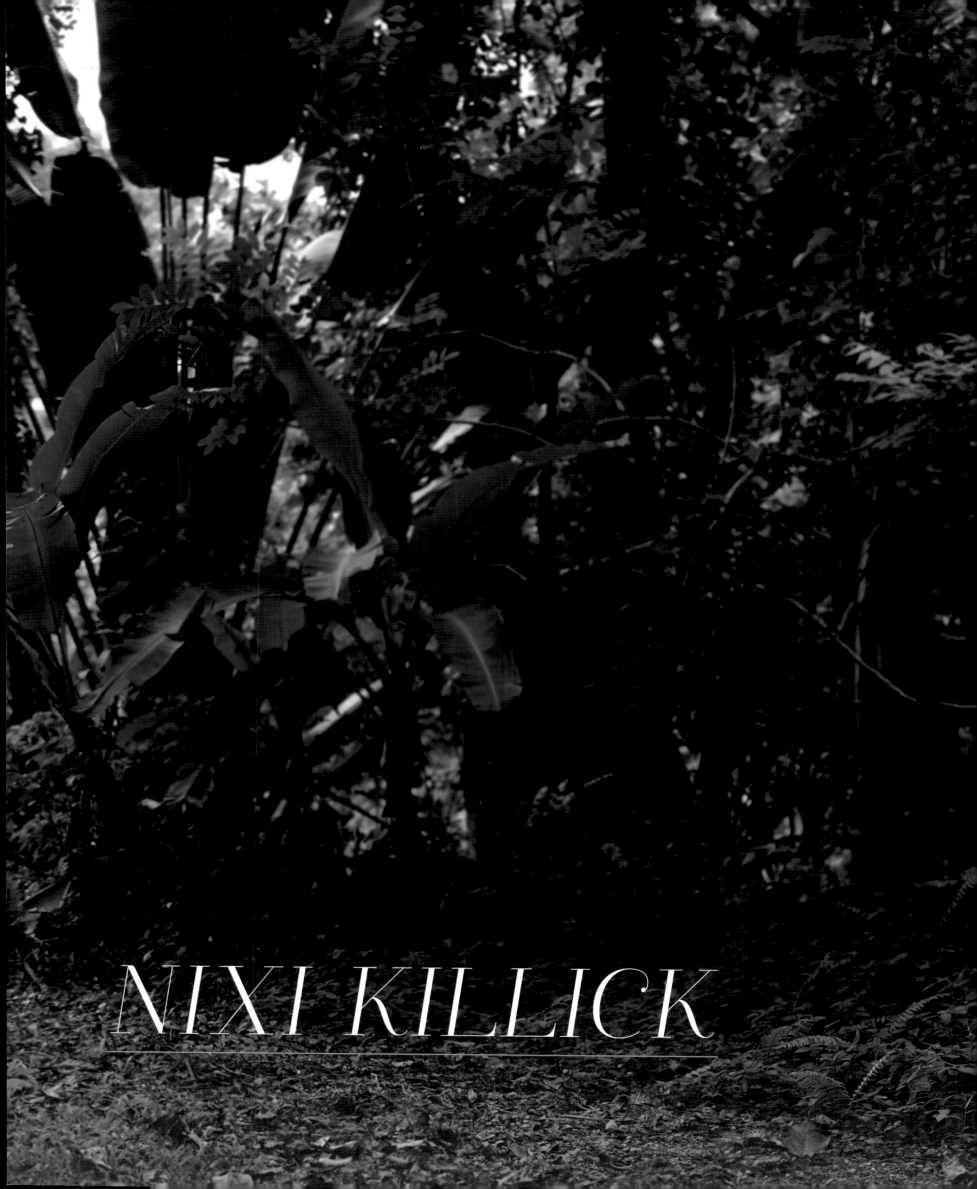

NIXI KILLICK

BY LIZ OHANESIAN

Raised in New South Wales by artist parents, Nixi Killick spent her formative years in the circus, where she performed acrobatics, twirled fire, and walked on stilts. She made costumes too. In the midst of a very practical pursuit—after all, a performer needs attire that's functional and eye-catching—the seeds of what would become Killick's artistic calling were sewn.

Today, Killick makes fashion that stands as conceptual art and manifests in individual pieces that mold to and flow around the body, where the design becomes a canvas for color to play and for intricate patterns to take shape. Her clothing is sculptural and painterly art for the body.

Killick describes herself as an "Imaginer," integrating multiple artistic disciplines into her practice to realize her creative visions. "I don't see things as clothes in a way," she explains. "The beginning is all about painting and trying to channel a story."

For Killick, those stories often delve into the intersection of nature and technology. "I'm always jostling with this idea of future primitive," she says. That shows in the presentations of her work. Killick works with collaborators—like photographer Robert Earp and make-up and special effects artist Lizzie Sharp—to bring the designs to life in visual stories that humanity's connection to nature with a sci-fi edge. Killick thinks of "the most radical future and the most incredible techno-optimist vision" in the conception of her work and that shines through in the finished collections where technology and nature live side-by-side harmoniously on garments.

You can see this melding of ideas in the presentation of her collections. In *Echo Echo*, from 2015, models with brightly painted faces complementing their multi-hued outfits pose against a nearly barren desert backdrop. Shades of yellow, pink and blue contrast against the white sand and dry brown plants around them. In *Meta-Flora* from 2014, the models pose against succulents and the images are altered so that the humans appear to shrink against the plant life. "Those shoots are really about creating the world that the collection represents, in a full kind of sense," she says.

"I'M ALWAYS JOSTLING WITH THIS IDEA OF FUTURE PRIMITIVE."

PREVIOUS SPREAD, OPPOSITE: Photo by Robert Earp. ABOVE: Photo by Aiichrio Uno.
FOLLOWING SPREAD (L-R): Photo by Melissa Cowan. Photo by Robert Earp.
2ND FOLLOWING SPREAD (L-R): Photo by Melissa Cowan. Photo by Robert Earp.
3RD FOLLOWING SPREAD (L-R): Photo by Ivanna Oksenyuk. Photo by Robert Earp.

215

"YOU HAVE TO BE ABLE TO DO ALL THESE TRICKS AND YOU HAVE TO LOOK FABULOUS AT THE SAME TIME."

More recently, the *Digital Drift* collection looks at both technology and environmental concerns, including the dire situation of the Great Barrier Reef. The concept plays out in shades of purple and blue. On a set of sleeves, a wildly intricate series of prints moves from brings together references to both the computer world and the sea. On leggings, a *Tron*-like grid is paired with shapes that conjure images of fish and seashells.

Technology has shaped Killick's designs in literal ways. She has laser cut medical-grade thermoplastics and 3-D printed pieces. Like painting, the process of making these more technology-driven pieces is part of the concept.

Killick's work is split between sculptural, wearable art and sportswear that is both accessible and clever. Killick's clothes are frequently made to move. These are the kind of outfits that make a statement at nightclubs, raves, and music festivals, but they're also designed to keep the wearer from becoming a wallflower. Items like maxi T-shirts, hot pants and the flowing "rave robe," are made for movement, but you'll still look like you're wearing a painting.

"With the streetwear level, the scene has to be just as wild, just as colorful, just as crazy, but really comfortable and they need to last you forever," she explains. "It's trying to translate across that so that you can have a piece that can really translate across your life and be part of all these different areas and maintain its brightness and maintain it's comfort, but you feel like you got dressed. That comes with the experience of being in the circus as well and having costumes that have to work when you're doing acrobatics and performance. You have to be able to do all these tricks and you have to look fabulous at the same time. They have to function properly, but also need to be as radical as possible."

From concept to completion, Killick's fashion is not just about her vision, but of connecting with the end user. "Being able to treat things as art in their conceptual depth, but make them accessible in a fashion platform means that in a way, you can have this conversation that's really personal and, really, a conceptual exploration of color fields and of different content," she says. "You can take that discussion and build that into something that people can feel a part of."

She adds, "The conversations that I have with people now who wear the things, it's amazing."✦

PREVIOUS SPREAD, OPPOSITE: Photo by Robert Earp.
THIS PAGE, TOP: Photo by Ivanna Oksenyuk.
THIS PAGE, RIGHT: Photo by Robert Earp.

OLGA
NORONHA

BY SILKE TUDOR

In 2010, when Olga Noronha was barely twenty years old, she exhibited an early suite titled *Dirty Tissues*, which included an atmospheric video and a ring fixed with a tiny silver box used to dispense tissues. The work, both impish and refined, sought to turn the "*so repulsive* act of blowing the nose" into the pinnacle of elegance. It was recognized by faculty at Central Saint Martins College of Art and Design as a significant and germinal work, and the prestigious London fashion school swiftly integrated *Dirty Tissues* into their permanent collection. They were not misguided.

In recent years, Noronha's designs have made audiences weep, as was reported by *Time Out* after her 2016 tribute to the ornate, classical beauty of Portuguese filigree presented against a background of heartrending *fado* at ModaLisboa.

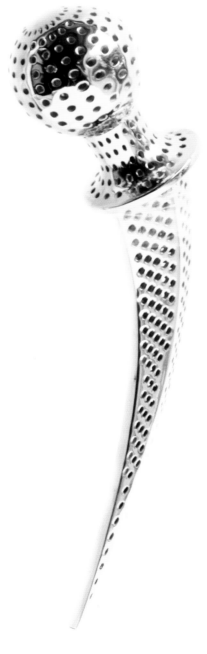

Noronha's designs have also made audiences gasp, as was heard when the lights went out during a recent runway show inspired by underwater bioluminescence (the centerpiece, a dress made from "stones" of polyester resin and photo-luminescent pigments, took Noronha two weeks to hand-assemble and weighed over nineteen pounds). Perhaps as often, though, Noronha's designs have made audiences squirm, as during her 2015 runway show in which flesh-colored gowns were cut off her models to reveal a network of sparkling arteries, veins, and capillaries; or the first time her models sauntered through Fashion Week wearing ornamental arm and neck braces.

"I do not want people to be apathetic towards my work, whatever their reaction—good or bad," says Noronha. "I wish for people to understand a piece of jewelry as more than a mere adornment. Aesthetics is far from the most important element; behind all my pieces there is an idea."

PREVIOUS SPREAD: Photo by Andre Brito.
OPPOSITE: "Nip & Tuck". Photo by Eliška Kyselková.
FOLLOWING SPREAD: (LEFT, TOP) Backstage shot. (BOTTOM) Photo by Anita Lisboa.
(RIGHT) Elbow restriction piece & knee restriction piece.

Incorporating unusual materials in her designs—real fish skin, hair, metal exoskeletons, fiber optics, coral-like barbs, and, most frequently, medical devices—Noronha routinely challenges traditional ideas of beauty and luxury (very few people look at ease in Noronha's designs). But even more challenging than her execution is Noronha's intention: to turn the human body into more than a canvas—to make the body, the flesh, the bones, the ligaments a critical medium with which her jewelry interacts.

In many ways this concept is not new to the fashion world in which everything from corsets to butt implants have served notions of high style, but Noronha's artistic interest in intimacy, integration, and inter-activity takes jewelry beyond the twenty-first century.

"My aim is then to question what jewelry is and what it can still be-come," wrote Noronha in *Humanity+*, a magazine which focuses on top-ics like transhumanism, nanotechnology, futurism, virtual reality, and brain-machine interfaces.

Initially inspired by her own aversion to needles, Noronha's ongoing project, *Medically Prescribed Jewelry*, had its beginnings in her father's orthopedic operating theater, where she pushed the boundaries of her own phobia by turning unused syringe and suture needles into earrings. Surprised by the similarities between the tools and techniques she saw used by jewelers and those used by her medically trained parents, Noronha went on to create staples and sutures out of precious met-als, a cervical collar out of exquisite gold filigree, and a series of artful braces and orthopedic supports which were splashed across European fashion magazines, including *Vogue* and *Elle*. The serviceable jewelry, which theoretically could offer clients the most intimate aesthetic choices of their lives, became her graduating project at CSM and has since evolved into a PhD thesis for Goldsmiths University of London,

a TED Talk, and a number of positions as teacher, guest lecturer, and, more recently, curator for a special collection at the Museo Del Gioiello Vicenza in Italy.

The pieces, themselves—from bejeweled orthodontics to prosthetic joints that are ornately carved or engraved with poetry—fall into four categories organized by their level of outward visibility: sub-dermal, exo-dermal, exo-corporeal, and intra-corporeal. That which can be seen, that which can be shown, that which can be felt, and that which can only be known.

The last category Noronha has described as hidden treasure.

Noronha is currently working with bioengineers and doctors to test the medical viability of her designs. If she has her way, physical limitation will provide the most profound avenue for radical self-expression, and, we will just have to speculate as to which passing body harbors the strangest and most beautiful jewels.

Forget tattoos, it's time to get that art inside of you.✛

"MY AIM IS THEN TO QUESTION WHAT JEWELRY IS AND WHAT IT CAN STILL BECOME."

PREVIOUS SPREAD: Photo by Carla Silva Pires.
OPPOSITE: Photo by Seth Solo.
THIS PAGE (CLOCKWISE): Photo by Carla Silva Pires, Prosthetic cervical collar & wrist restriction piece, Hip poem piece with Shakespeare inscription.

SASHA
FROLOVA

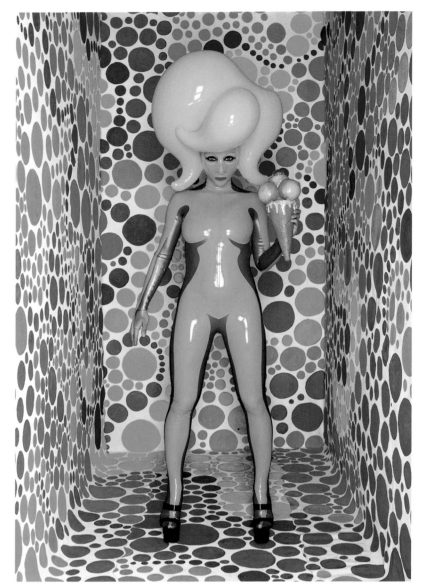

BY ANDY SMITH

Sasha Frovola does more than just create synthetic worlds bursting with color and pop. The Moscow designer puts on the latex herself and acts as its ambassador. She's the one taking the microphone—made at times to look like an enormous ice cream cone or lipstick—and leading the performance art/musical project *Aquaaerobika*. Referring to herself as a "live sculpture" in this form, Frovola acts as a self-described "universal superwoman from the future with ultra-abilities," and with each performance among her inflatables and backup performers, the audience is offered just a peek into Frovola's vibrant vision.

Aquaaerobika, with its electro-pop sounds and Bauhaus sensibilities, is just another extension of Frovola's practice, which moves through sculpture, design, fashion, and performance art. She's chasing *gesamtkunstwerk*, a term coined by writer and philosopher K.F.E. Trahndorff to describe a single work of art comprised of many (or even all) art disciplines at once. She describes the plot of the *Aquaaerobika* live show as "an endless travel through parallel worlds of future," but each of her projects seem to revel in this concept in uniting varying arts. The thirty-three-year-old has spent more than a decade building her professional career crafting this aesthetic.

Within the art world, one looks at Frovola's inflatable sculptures and installations and might consider the work of Jeff Koons, an artist sometimes cited as an influence for her. Yet, Frovola

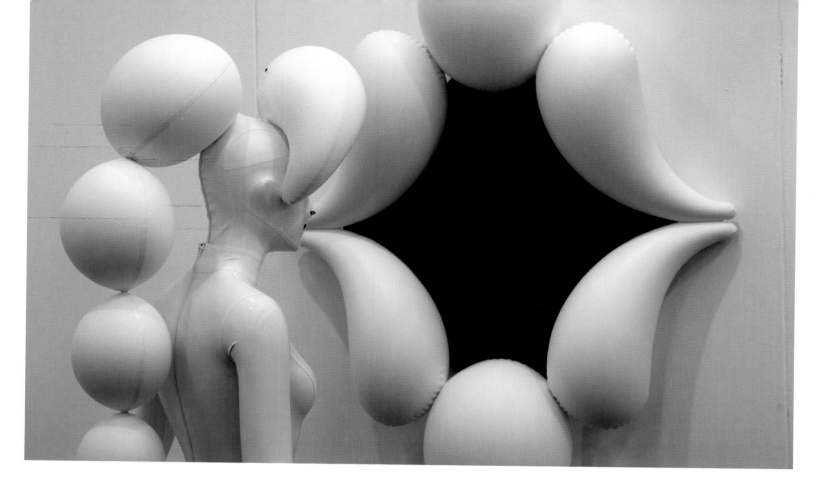

isn't recreating objects otherwise seen as banal; she isn't fabricating known artifacts via unpredictable means. She's not even attempting to ground the viewer in anything familiar at all. These are *manga*-like experiences in the flesh—packed with towering, faux hairdos, form-fitting suits, and Super Soaker palettes. Berlin's Norwind Festival described her shows as "Oskar Schlemmer's Triadic Ballet meets Lady Gaga." She's pulling from retro sci-fi, Japanese pop culture, eight-bit video games, and psychedelia—a chimera of niche fantasies. Yet, somehow, what's presented is a distinct landscape of another time and place.

Her sculptural practice has taken her work to New Holland in Saint Petersburg, the Moscow Museum of Modern Art, Aidan Gallery in Moscow, the Moscow Biennale of Contemporary Art, and elsewhere. In the context of her larger body of work, her sculptures appear as vessels with which her living sculptures can travel. They appear as interdimensional objects against contemporary backdrops. She's added components of augmented reality and projections to take her work even further beyond what can be expected.

And while she's become an international name, Frovola is a product of Moscow schools. She's a graduate of the Stroganov Moscow State University of Arts and Industry, the National Institute of Design, and the Institute for Problems of Contemporary Art. She was a finalist for the Kandinsky Prize 2009 in the "Young Artist / Project of the Year" category and later, was also a finalist for the Arte Laguna Prize 12.13 in Venice. It was in 2006 that Frovola and friends started throwing *Aquaaerobika* parties after fashion shows in Moscow. In an interview with the magazine *Gay & Night*, she described the parties as having a swimsuit dress code and a "vivid, wild cocktail of wet, naked bodies, glitter, champagne, makeup, eyelashes longer than heels, lots of light and music." In the winter season, she and her friends were playing on the tropes of '80s style, aerobics, and the pool party. When she wanted to write a theme song for one of the parties, she began a path that saw her take *Aquaaerobika* parties to clubs and, eventu-

ally, major festivals. (Also credited as the current team behind the full *Aquaaerobika projec*t are sound director/composer Kenmee, composers Tolik Tyler, Aerobika, and Poko Cox, and collaborative songwriter Gosha Rubchinsky.)

Frovola, under the name Miss Zero +, entered the famed Alternative Miss World Contest in London once again in 2014, after participating in previous years. The event, open to contestants of any gender, is a flamboyant affair celebrating Avant-Garde fashion, drag culture, and anything "alternative." Alternative Miss World has the categories of day-wear, evening dresses, swimwear, and an interview of its mainstream counterpart and Frovola obliged with her synthetic style. The event was started by British sculptor/performance artist/ jeweler Andrew Logan in 1972, and even among some of the most wild ensembles imaginable, Frovola's skintight, shiny costume stood out. That year, she won the crown. "It gets extremely hot inside the costume," she told the Daily Mail at the time. "I have to wear it for three hours at a time and all I change is the mask, but I love the

"IT GETS EXTREMELY HOT INSIDE THE COSTUME... BUT I LOVE THE WAY IT LOOKS. I FEEL LIKE A PLASTIC WOMAN."

OPPOSITE:
Photo: Irina Voiteleva, 2009.

ABOVE:
"The Bride". Installation.
Inflatable latex sculpture. Art Brussels Art Fair. 2011
Photo: Ivan Onoprienko, Irina Voiteleva.

FOLLOWING SPREAD:
"Lyubolet", inflatable latex
sculpture and two aliens suits.
Performance documentation.
Photo: Anna Pitich, 2008.

2ND FOLLOWING SPREAD:
(LEFT, TOP): Portrait in front of Love-Me-Blaster
sculpture. "Cyberprincess" exhibition view. Photo:
Vladimir Maximov, 2009. (LEFT, BOTTOM) The Bow.
Inflatable latex sculpture. From "Albinism" series,
2010. Photo: Anna Pitich. (RIGHT) Aquaaerobika.
Photo: Irina Voiteleva, 2015.

PREVIOUS SPREAD:
Aquaaerobika *performance.*
Photo: Carina Okula, 2015.

THIS PAGE, TOP:
"Paradizarium" exhibition view.
PERMM Museum of Contemporary
Art, Perm, Russia. 2017 Photo:
Max Kimerling.

ABOVE:
"Twirl". Inflatable latex
sculpture, 2016.

OPPOSITE:
Photo from Paradizarium *series.*
Irina Voiteleva &
Sasha Frolova, 2017.

way it looks. I feel like a plastic woman. People should know that I am not a fetishist though, it is not a sexual thing for me; it is for performance art."

Frovola's point about not being a fetishist is particularly interesting, as her work is often given that descriptor alongside allusions to children's toys and *anime.* In spring 2017, her *Inflandia* exhibition at Luftmuseum in Germany brought her vision inside the walls of the institution. Her massive inflatable sculptures, past costumes, and murals depicting her characters filled a Luftmuseum gallery, and in a video interview with the museum, she touched on what she sees as her themes: "[It's] some kind of fantastic land, full of magic shapes and bright col-

ors," she said. "This is a version of the future that maybe will come someday. This is my own parallel reality, where I want to invite people. I think every artist should create his own parallel world in which he speaks his own visual language, so my objects and my shapes and my songs, all that you will see in the exhibition, is the way I'm speaking about the future, about love, and what's important to me. And this is the language I'm speaking to the artist, the language of my art, my emotions, my fantasy." In past interviews, she's said she fell in love with latex at first sight. She says it was not only the otherworldliness of the material, but the aliveness of it. Above all, she acknowledges and seems to enjoy the dualities of latex: It seems unnatural,

but it's found in nature. It can appear hard, yet feel soft. And yes, there is sometimes a sexual connotation with it—yet in another moment, there's something youthful and innocent in the material. That tension carries into the evocations of her sculptures, music, and broader infiltration of the viewer's senses.

Collectively, latex, movement, inflatables, and disco-house music is Frovola's vessel in relating her alternate world. And while we, as viewers, will continue to extract our own themes and meanings out of her vibrant experiences, we're simply visitors to an alien world and Frovola is the only "universal superwoman" who can take us there. +

TANEL VEENRE

BY ANDY SMITH

I n the hands of Estonia-born artist Tanel Veenre, the idea of jewelry becomes something otherworldly. Whether it's his elaborate, translucent "crowns" or bestial neckwear, the designer has forged new possibilities out of familiar concepts. What asked what influences this type of work, Veenre appropriately corrects the notion that he does just one thing: "I am not sure what you mean by *this* kind of work," he says. "I am doing whimsical fashion jewellery in thousands of copies, unique and profound art jewellery pieces, and quick body pieces for stage presence. They all have very different paths and influences. [But] sometimes a painting I see in the museum or a bird singing behind my window can make a major impact to what I will create next. I live with an open heart."

Sure enough, Veenre's work diverges even from its own history. During our conversation, he mentions several bodies of work currently in process—"sleek erotic forms, juicy Christian crosses, dark seahorses with golden bubbles"—and how even he doesn't know his end destination. This "organic" approach to his work carries broadly over into his life, he says. This means that some project take five to seven years come to to fruition, while others appear nearly spontaneously. And the different functions of his jewelry calls for different modes of showcase. Some of his work is intended to be shown on stages; some of it is sold directly through galleries like Ornamentum in the U.S., Sweden's Platina, Latvia's PUTTI, or

Reverso in Portugal. The latter type seems to demand the most attention and craftsmanship.

Tanel Veenre Jewelery (TVJ) comes with the slogan "Kingdom of Dreams." There's a whimsical, yet stark quality that carries across these works. At home, the line has become a favorite of First Lady of Estonia Evelin Ilves, E.U. High Representative Federica Mogherini, and popstar Kerli Kõiv. Elsewhere, the pieces appear in *Vogue*, *L'Officiel*, and *W Magazine*. Inside the cufflinks and bangles are touches of the fantastic, small animals, and a unexpected elegance.

OPPOSITE: Headpiece, hand-cut PVC.
ABOVE (L-R): Neckpiece "Before the Sunset",
wood, silver, cosmic dust.
Neckpiece "Primal Scream III", reconstructed coral,
silicone, wood, cosmic dust.

FOLLOWING SPREAD (L-R):
"Book of Fears"
necklace, carved jet, fluorite, wool, silver.
Headpiece, hand-cut PVC.

2ND FOLLOWING SPREAD:
(LEFT) "Cosmic Headpiece" (RIGHT, CLOCKWISE
FROM LEFT) Neckpiece "Primal Scream I", recon-
structed coral, silicone, wood, cosmic dust.
Neckpiece "Big Trophy", wood, silver, cosmic dust.

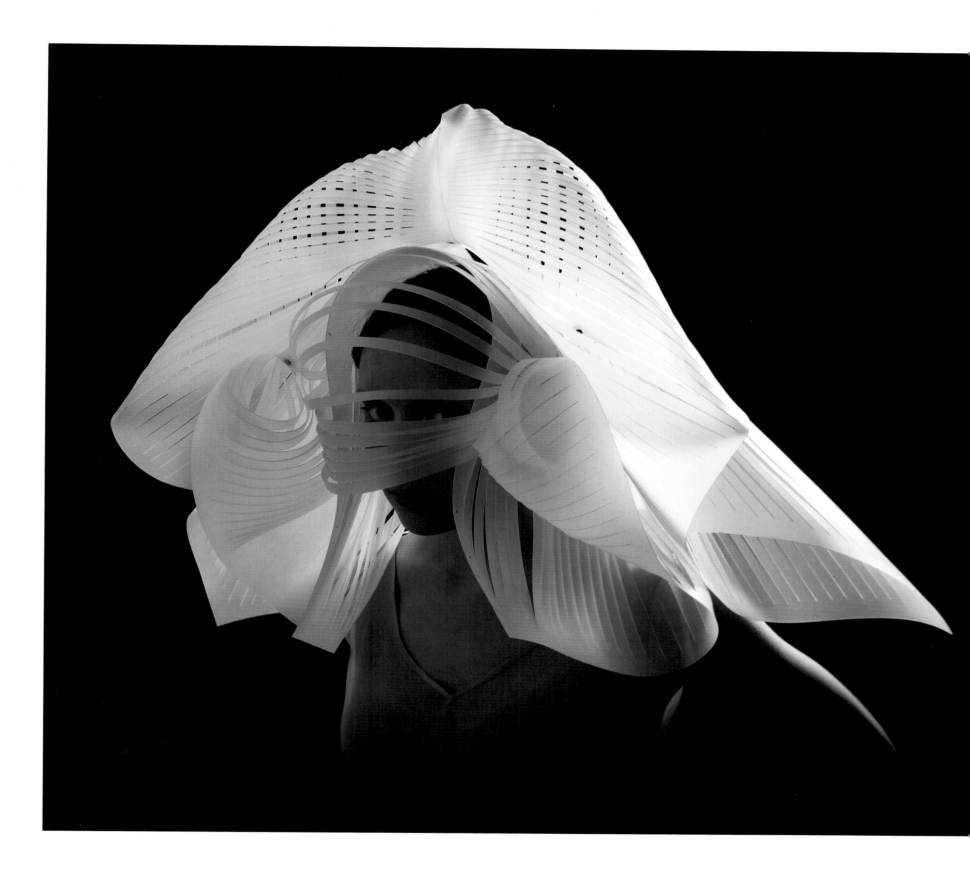

Veenre counts friends who are also fashion designers and photographers as influences and also, Kadri Mälk. Mälk is a professor of jewelry at Estonian Academy of Art, and Veenre credits him with "a lot of drama and boldness to my works." However, the longest-standing motivators in the designer's life would be his family—a band of musicians and artists. "I think kindness and supportiveness of my parents has been a major influence," he offers. "They let me grow rather organically, they trusted my choices so it's easier for my now as well to trust myself. And I want to give this knowledge to my kids, I wanna hear them growing and just supporting them in their natural choices. Human beings are beautiful, we shouldn't forget that."

And though his works can appear entirely alien, the natural world is a major part of the engine that drives Veenre's imagination. It's both a tactile and an abstract factor in the designer's ouput: "The sea is the eternity, openness to unlimited possibilities," he says. "As a dreamer, I like to fly away. Nature in general has been my major influence through materials I use. So it's more like a dialogue; nature teaches me the logic of organic forms. How to grow as an artist, how to make your pieces to grow similar way as I see the patterns from nature. And I just love carving wood, to feel it's friendly warmth in my hands."

In an occupational sense, Veenre also moves between his work as a freelance artist, a designer behind his celebrated brand TVJ, and now being a professor at the Estonian Academy of Arts. He maintains that he's "addicted to the euphoria of freedom." So with more than one-hundred-fifty solo and group exhibitions, ever-growing

lines of jewelry and projects, a teaching career, and a presence in in his native Estonia, the U.S., Spain, Italy, China, Finland, Sweden, Mexico, and so many other countries comes a question: What exactly is he trying to accomplish? "Hmmm ...," he starts. "First I would like to have peace with myself. It's about completing my soul. But as a social animal, I would like to touch people, to make them less broken and more as a whole. And I would like to encourage them to dream—it's good for your heart."✛

"...SOMETIMES A PAINTING I SEE IN THE MUSEUM OR A BIRD SINGING BEHIND MY WINDOW CAN MAKE A MAJOR IMPACT TO WHAT I WILL CREATE NEXT."

OPPOSITE: Headpiece, "The Crown", wood, cosmic dust
ABOVE: Headpiece, hand cut PVC.
PREVIOUS SPREAD:
(LEFT) Neckpiece "Wreath of Victory",
wood, silver, cosmic dust. (RIGHT)Headpiece, hand cut PVC.

AGNIESZKA
OSIPA

BY ANDY SMITH

A glance at one of Agnieszka Osipa's costumed goddesses, defiant in her grace and power, recalls an old Slavic poem, as translated by author James Bailey:

In body she's like a swan's wing,
Her walk is like that of a doe with golden horns.
Her face is like white snow,
Her eyes are like those of a bright falco,
Her brows are like black sable—
There shouldn't be another such woman in this world.

A thousand years after the Slavic mythology was venerated by early Eastern Europeans, costume designer Agnieszka Osipa counts the traditions and narratives of this culture as a primary influence in her works. This accounts for the hundreds and hundreds of beads adorning her headpieces, each following a tradition of meticulous art paying homage to gods and goddesses.

This Polish artist was born in 1986, in the tiny town of Nowa Sarzyna. An early interest in painting was fostered at The Higher School of Art and Design in Poland. And after further study at the Academy of Fine Arts in Łódz and the urging from a professor, she pivoted to fashion. "The path I pursued was unusual I think," she says. "I've always made paintings even though I was studying in the field of fashion. I [hadn't] sewn much during the five years. The costumes were in my life only after I finished the education and had to figure out what to do and what to pursue. Looking back at the decision, I think it was a good one."

Today, her process ended up being a blend of how one would approach fashion design and freeform painting. There's an active transformation occurring in each work that Osipa designs to meet her own imagination. "Only the custom orders are made by design that is sketched earlier," she shares. "As for my own work, [it's] very chaotic ... For example, it's quite common for a corset to become a headpiece or the other way around, just because the form's outcome is not planned at all. In the process, I am watching movies and listening to music and tend to swim away from conscious decision making and the designs just happen."

"...IT'S QUITE COMMON FOR A CORSET TO BECOME A HEADPIECE OR THE OTHER WAY AROUND, JUST BECAUSE THE FORM'S OUTCOME IS NOT PLANNED AT ALL."

PREVIOUS SPREAD: Photo by Bella Kotak. OPPOSITE: Photo by Marcin Nagraba.
ABOVE: Photo by Ekaterina Belinskaya.
FOLLOWING SPREAD (L-R): Photos by Marcin Nagraba, Ekaterina Belinskaya.

"I USE LEATHER RIGHT NEXT TO PLASTIC, THE MATERIALS ARE NOT AS IMPORTANT AS THE FORMS THEY ALLOW ME TO CREATE."

The music emitting from her speakers are also blends: folk metal, ambient pagan, and the multi-genre sounds of ensembles like Da-khaBrakha. ("Most of all it's folklore music from the Slavic culture, Slavic mythology, and themes of dark macabre in fairy tales from the region," she says.) Osipa cites music as a primary influence. In various interviews, including the one for this piece, she is able to rattle off names of acts currently inspiring her: Pagan folk-metal act Svarga, neo-folk rockers Krynitza, and several others. Medieval-folk act Faun even used Osipa costumes for the cover of its 2014 record *Luna*. A trip to the "post-folk" music festival Menuo Juoda-ragis is the type of galvanizing outings that takes Osipa to her next project.

Each of these bands and performers is part of a necessary element as she crafts each intricate crest, bodypiece, and seemingly endless gowns that extend a model's body to godlike proportions. And the times on these sessions vary: "For headpieces, it takes around a week of time to make," she offers. "As for costumes or corsets it varies from two weeks to two months, depending on the complexity."

Osipa says the models aren't often on her mind during the creation of each costume and accessory. ("I do not tend to focus on the model in the process of making the costume, I leave this aspect to the photographers to decide," she says.) Yet, it's still notable that the individuals outfitted in Osipa's deity-inspired works range in age and demographics, distancing her pieces from the ever-youthful fantasy cosplay and, in many cases, accenting their antique sensibilities.

That and those other seemingly authentic qualities of Osipa's costumes are hard earned. It's a painstaking process, in terms of not

only sheer labor but also acquiring just the right ingredients. "The challenges are mainly in getting the materials needed," she says. "The ideas were always with me. Basically I have more concepts in my head than time to make them. That also might be seen as a challenge. There are also crazy work hours from time to time, because most of my clients have very short timeframes for orders. So it happens that I work fourteen to sixteen hours a day."
Those materials vary greatly, piece to piece. When *Trend Tablet* asked the artist for specifics, she offered this insight: "When I use many materials so it's truly hard to pinpoint one. I use leather right next to plastic, the materials are not as important as the forms they allow me to create."

The backdrops used to display Osipa's costumes also vary, in photographs of models bearing Osipa's work. The figures stand against snowy forests, intricate ballrooms, moody, black backgrounds, and whitewashed settings resembling the afterlife. The models are posed stoic or threatening, tortured or holding divine dominion. They lay on funeral pyres, in mourning, mid-ceremony, or triumphant. All seem to be on a journey, a reflection of their epic natures. Each photographer is able to activate her costumes in a different way, yet all carry the attribute of story.

That opportunity for narrative isn't just reserved for fashion photographers. Osipa has lent her designs to the world of live music, as well. The German dark metal band Sariola employed the services of Osipa for the members' stage costumes. Finnish metal bands Ensiferum and Insomnium have followed suit. All of these acts attempt to tap into the mythological nature of their genre: Osipa aids in helping transport audiences to the fictional, ancient worlds they reference. Yet, the same resume that carries these clients also is filled with fashion magazine covers and mainstream acknowledge-

ABOVE: Photo by Marcin Nagraba.
OPPOSITE (TOP LEFT): Photo by Ekaterina Belinskaya.
OPPOSITE (ALL OTHERS): Photos by Marcin Nagraba.
FOLLOWING SPREAD (L-R): Photos by Marcin Nagraba.

"I HAVE MORE CONCEPTS IN MY HEAD THAN TIME TO MAKE THEM..."

ments. She's helped design multiple fashion spreads for the publication *Dark Beauty Magazine*, which says it's "dedicated to artists, fashion designers, photographers, musicians, and actors who crave dark glamour."

Viewers have a particular fascination with the headpieces created by the artist. Recent creations dance around themes of witchcraft: The title of one skeletal crown, "Malleus Maleficarum," references the so-called "Hammer of Witches," a Catholic treatise that condones the murder of witches. The series "Pagan Poetry" further shows Osipa's fascination with the heathens of the Old and New worlds. Yet, even the natural world can prove an influence: "DANDELION (*dmuchawiec*)"—with its pearls, ornaments, and embroidery—takes on a form quite similar to its floral counterpart.

Osipa's collaborations are the primary in which the world sees her pieces. She has worked with photographers like Marcin Nagraba (who often uses his own mother to model Osipa's pieces) and A.M. Lorek. The latter shooter has much in common with Osipa: They share first names, home countries, a love for music, and most importantly, an ability to create magic with tangible tools.

Sorting out the specifics of how Osipa helps photographers create these worlds—just like the exact materials she uses or their intended uses, once finished—takes away from the supernatural quality of Osipa's work. Rather, the artist's designs are based and relayed in metaphors and mythological terms, much like the feats of the heroes, heroines, gods, goddesses, demonesses, and witches that populate her imagination as she toils away each day. It's when you're confronted with these pieces—taking your view away from this world and into a time long forgotten—that the magic of Osipa's work is fully realized. ✦

ABOVE: Photo by Sheridan's Art.
LEFT: Photo by Marcin Nagraba.
OPPOSITE: Photo by Agnieszka Lorek.
1ST FOLLOWING SPREAD (L-R):
Photo by Agnieszka Lorek, Photo by Marcin Nagraba.
2ND FOLLOWING SPREAD (L-R):
Photo by Ekaterina Belinskaya,
Photo by Marcin Nagraba.

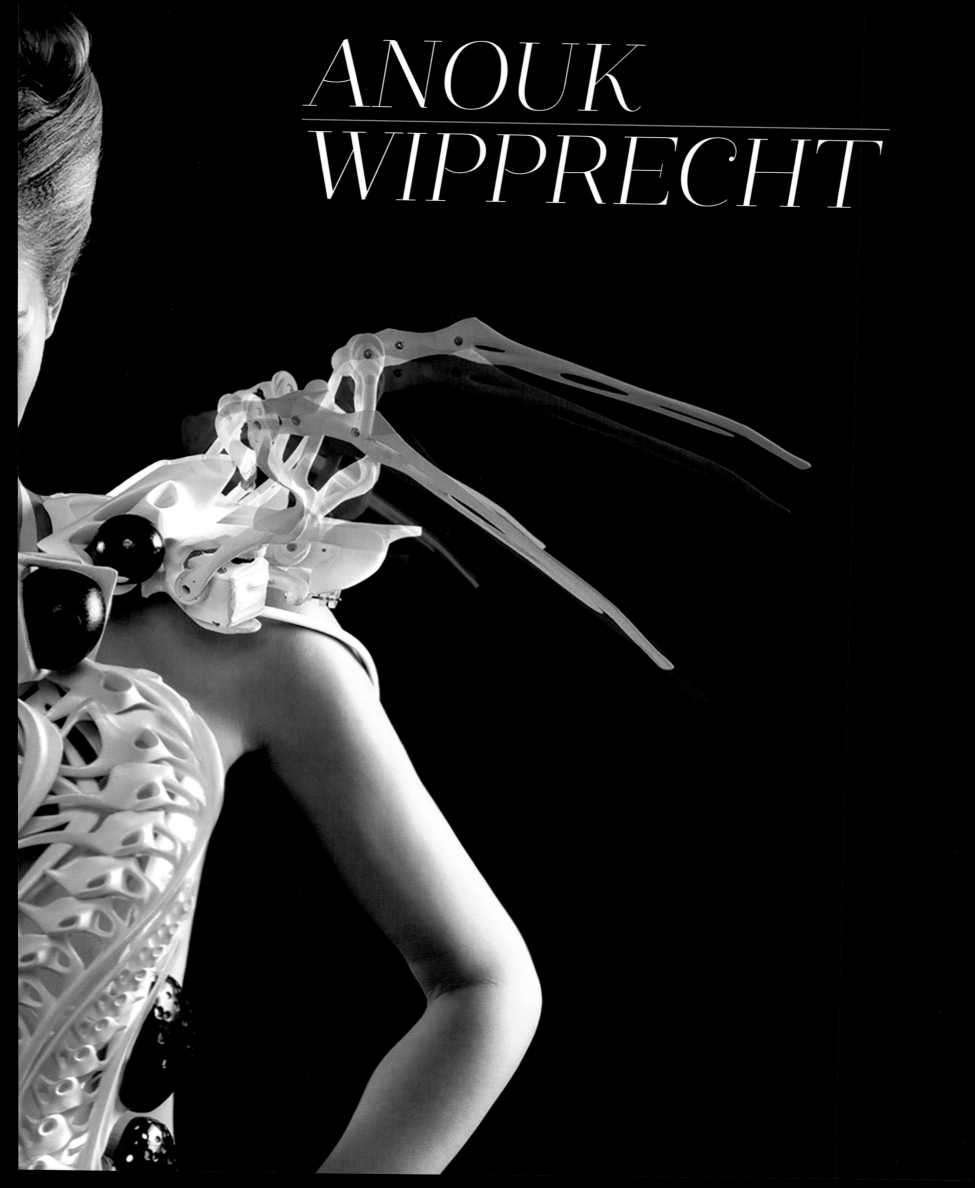

ANOUK
WIPPRECHT

BY ANDY SMITH

Traveling between San Francisco, Los Angeles, and Amsterdam, designer Anouk Wipprecht is not only traveling through hemispheres, but also industries. She works in the burgeoning field of "Fashion-Tech," which she defines as "a rare combination of fashion design combined with engineering, science, and interaction/user-experience design." This means that Wipprecht's garments are laced with computing components and sensors, which monitor both the space surrounding the wearer and the levels of comfort inside his or her body. Her collaborators range from computer hardware companies to crystal producer Swarovski.

The most famous example of Wipprecht's ambition so far is the "Spider Dress." It's a garment that garnered international headlines for both its emotional and physical implications. The three-dimensionally printed *couture*, outfitted with sensors and powered by Intel Edison technology, has animatronic legs that react when passers-by get too close to the wearer or adapt to her desires. Simply, Wipprecht says, the dress "acts as the interface between the body and the external world."

Wipprecht's design practice poses one, big question: "What does fashion lack?" Her answer: "Microcontrollers." It's certainly not the first response most would give in the broader industry of fashion. But for this designer, the tiny, powerful devices are the key to the future. "The relationship between the body and technology is closer than ever since designers, artists, scientists, and engineers started combining their practices at the beginning of this century, and with every passing day we are weaving electronics more tightly into the fabric of our physical world," her studio says. "Electronic systems can now be layered seamlessly onto a material or substrate such as plastic or polyester. Embedded processors and sensors for transmitting and receiving information create a vision of cultural transformation that is both exciting and disturbing."

Her innovations have led to partnerships with Google, Microsoft, Intel, AutoDesk, Cirque Du Soleil, Audi, and Materialise, a company centered on 3-D printing. Wipprecht brings a vision for how to integrate new technologies into garments while knowing how to create pieces that would otherwise be considered high fashion. The "Spider Dress" is noted for both its technology and its fierce aesthetics. A partnership with Audi, debuting at Berlin Fashion Week in 2015, saw four dresses that used technology found within the company's A4 saloon car. Two dresses in the set had flashing parking sensors for close objects. Another beared sixty-watt, headlight-like LEDs that blinded, and the last dress's surface allowed for projection mapping, giving the illusion of motion.

PREVIOUS SPREAD:
"Spider Dress" by Anouk Wipprecht.
Photo by Jason Perry.

OPPOSITE:
Photo by Anouk Wipprecht.
ABOVE: Photo by Jason Perry.

FOLLOWING SPREAD, LEFT: "Smoke Dress". Photo by Michiel Kivits. (RIGHT): "Smoke Dress". Model: Viktoria Modesta. Photo by Nhu Xuan Hua.

2ND and 3RD FOLLOWING SPREADS: Photos by Jason Perry. 4TH FOLLOWING SPREAD (L-R): Photo by Allan Amato. Photo by Marije Dijkema.

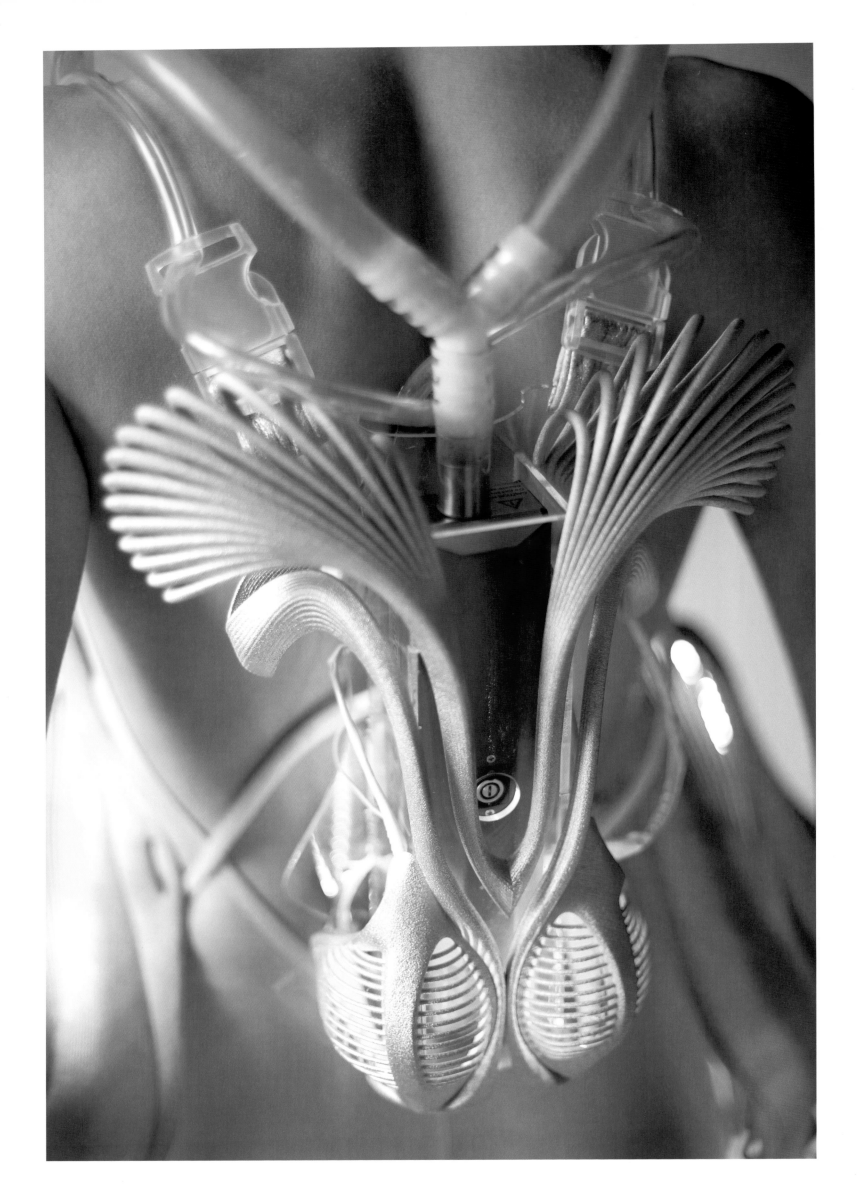

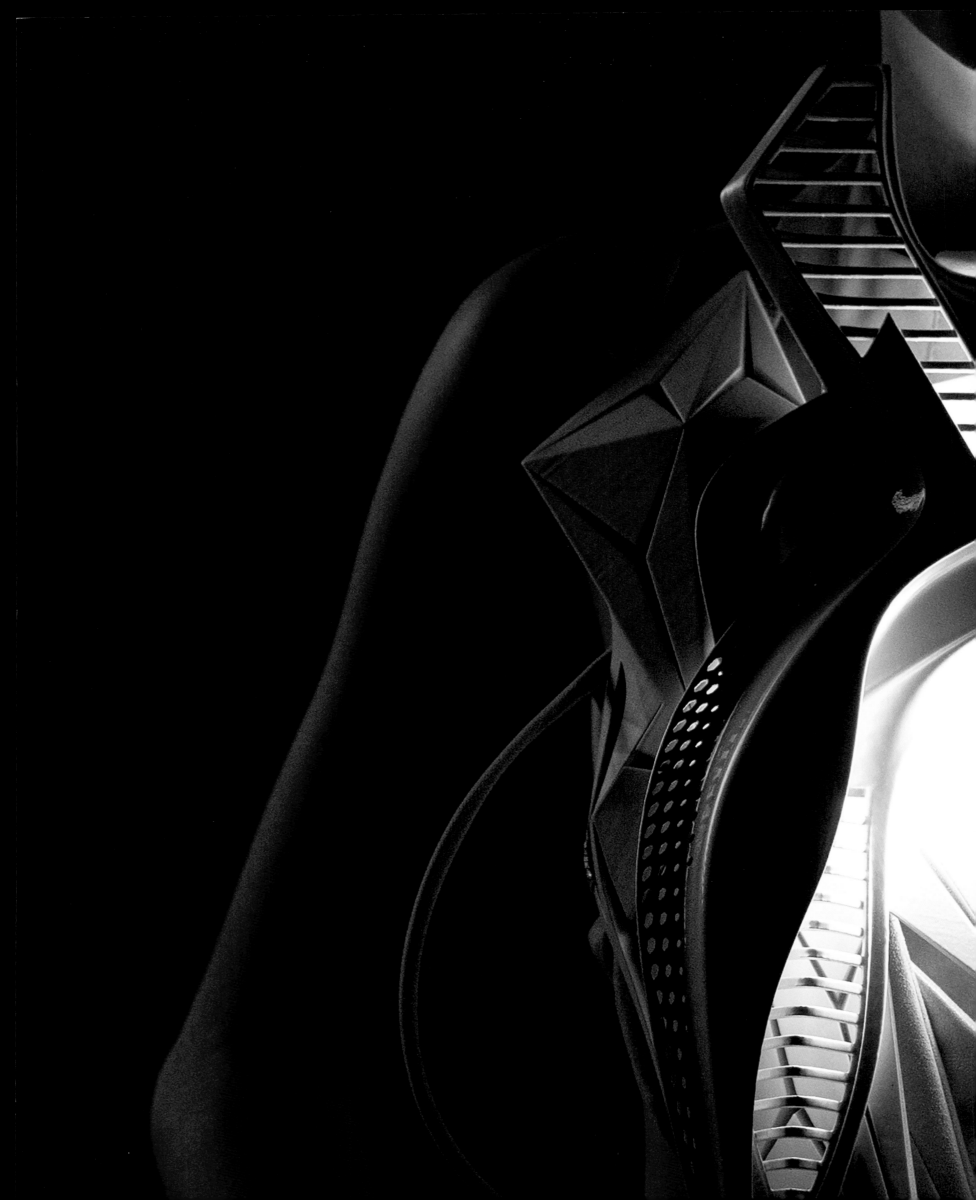

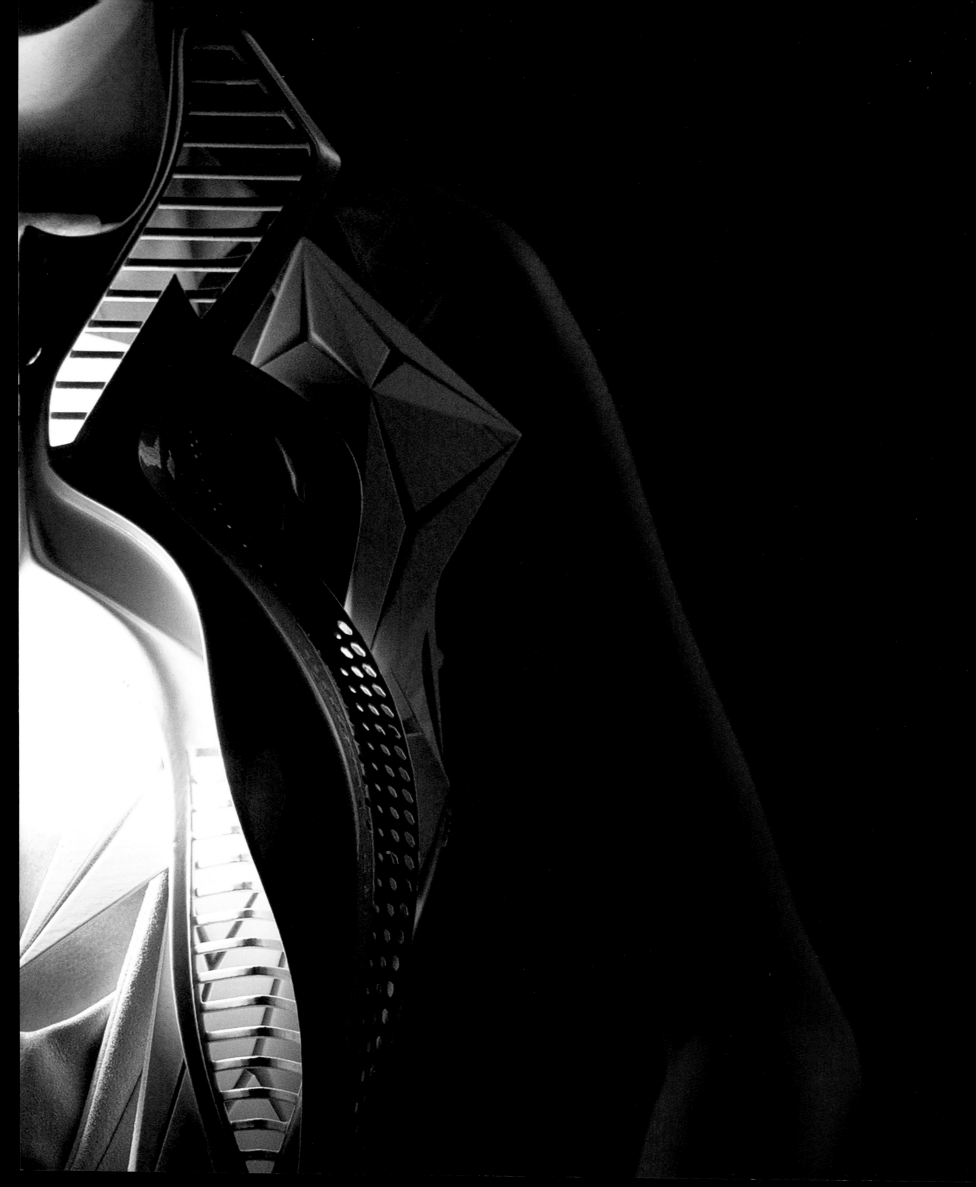

"THE RELATIONSHIP BETWEEN THE BODY AND TECHNOLOGY IS CLOSER THAN EVER..."

Many see fashion as an outlet for self-expression, and in a physical sense, it's difficult to imagine a more personal collection of garments than those crafted by Wipprecht. She's created pieces that flash in time with the wearer's heartbeat. A headpiece created through her collaborations tracks the attention level of a wearer and a camera on its front captures the scene whenever the wearer is most tense, allowing a database of triggers. In yet another showcase of the designer's ability to mix fields, this unicorn-shaped headpiece created at the Sparks Project brings in electroencephalography (or EEG), monitoring brain activity usually reserved for the medical sector. As Next Nature Network puts it, this project could help "children with autism learn how their brains work, to handle situations that make them uncomfortable."

A majority of Wipprecht's recent projects seem to be centered on the emotional comfort of the wearer. That's not a new concept in fashion, but it's rarely been tackled on the levels the designer's work seems to be unlocking. Wipprecht's "Smoke Dress" pushes out a veil of smoke when a person gets too close, while her "Synapse Dress" logs your mood throughout the day. Her robotic creations end up taking an animalistic personality in how they protect the person inside the dress. In a sense, there are many classical fashion concepts at play, yet amplified. A dress made by Wipprecht can help one feel empowered and comfortable on several levels.

It's difficult to imagine that you'll see a "Spider Dress" or "Smoke Dress" out in public any time soon. But as Wipprecht continues to innovate through her partnerships and technology continues to improve, one has to wonder if Wipprecht's vision for the future of fashion is much closer than it seems. ✦

ABOVE: "Smoke Dress". Photo by Michiel Kivits.
RIGHT: Anouk Wipprecht testing out her creation.
Photo by Marije Dijkema.
OPPOSITE: Anouk Wipprecht Audi project.

PREVIOUS SPREAD:
(LEFT, TOP) Anouk Wipprecht's Audi project.
(LEFT, BOTTOM) Photo by Jason Perry.
(RIGHT) "Spider Dress". Photo by Jason Perry.

CONTRIBUTORS

ATTABOY / EDITOR, DESIGNER

After graduating from the Fashion Institute of Technology (with a degree in Toy Design), Daniel "Attaboy" Seifert began a career of art, toy design, and performance poetry; until he accidentally co-founded *Hi-Fructose* in 2005 with his now wife, artist Annie Owens. Since then, *Hi-Fructose* has thrived as a publication and was honored with a ten year retrospective exhibition at the Virginia MOCA, the Akron Museum of Art, and the Crocker Art Museum. Atta has also authored several books for children and adult children, as well as co-created several animation properties, now locked in the vaults of Hollywood. Recently, he has begun to show his personal work publicly again as well as produce board games and other physical media projects for all the wrong reasons.

CARO BUERMANN / WRITER

Caro Buermann is a Los Angeles-based art curator and writer. In 2015, Caro was appointed the online editor of *Hi-Fructose*, before being named the new curator of Corey Helford Gallery in 2016. She also spent a large part of her career consulting with artists in Asia, where she manages Japanese figurative painter Hikari Shimoda. She regularly contributes to *Hi-Fructose Magazine* in print.

ANDY SMITH / WRITER

Andy Smith is a regular contributor to *Hi-Fructose Magazine* and the HiFructose.com blog. He lives in Charlotte, N.C., where he serves as digital editor and arts editor at Charlotte magazine. He's also written for publications like *Back Issue!*, *Weekly World News*, and *Outreach Magazine*. Reach him at andytalks.art.

SILKE TUDOR / WRITER

Silke Tudor is a freelance writer living in Philadelphia. She splits her time between the library, the docks, and a magical garden covered in broken glass.

ALINA CAMPBELL / INTRODUCTION

Alina Campbell left her Southern California roots behind to study fashion design at The Fashion Institute of Technology in New York City where she was influenced by the punk scene, street style, and vintage clothing in the East Village. She has spent the past twenty years as an independent fashion designer and costume archivist working for The Museum at FIT, Metropolitan Opera House Archive, FIDM Museum and Lucasfilm Archive. Her professional experience also includes designing costumes for videos and performances for Britney Spears, Mary J. Blige, Eve and Pink, among others. Having returned to California, she currently works at Skywalker Ranch as Senior Registrar, maintaining the costume collection for the Lucas Museum of Narrative Art.

JEFF D. MIN / WRITER

Jeff Min prefers bridges over walls. His ancestors are his silent guides, and his wife is a living reminder that the only thing that matters, in this life and the next, is love.

LIZ OHANESIAN / WRITER

Liz Ohanesian is a Los Angeles-based journalist who covers culture and arts. In addition to *Hi-Fructose*, she writes regularly for *L.A. Weekly*. She has also written for *Village Voice*, *Playboy*, *KCET Artbound*, and a number of other publications.

EVAN ROSA / COPY EDITOR

Evan Rosa has been Copyeditor for *Hi-Fructose Magazine* since Volume 8. He is a lifelong aficionado of art, music, and words, and is a proud member of the grammar police. He lives, breathes, and surfs in Southern California.

ADDITIONAL CREDITS:

COVER: *From the* White Collection *by Bea Szenfeld. Photo by Joel Rhodin.*
PAGE 1: *Leonid Titow. Photo by Maxim Gizatullin. Makeup artist: Svetlana Malaya.*
PAGE 2/ PAGE 297: *Flavia Rose. Detail of "Ester" concept.*
PAGE 3: *Sasha Frovola. Aquaaerobika. Photo: Wouter van Gens, 2016.*
PAGE 4: *Osipa Agnieszka. Photo by Ekaterina Belinskaya.*

PAGE 5: *Ana Rajevic. Photo by Fernando Lessa. Model: Anna Tatton.*
PAGE 7: *Sylwana Zybura. Jewellery Campaign for Xiyang Tang '17.*
PAGE 10: *Nikoline Liv Andersen. From* The Dance of the Deaf and Dumb Eye Exhibition *at Horsens Museum of Modern Art and Designmuseum Danmark, 2011-2012 Photographer Nicky de Silva.*
PAGE 11: *Dinu Bodiciu. "Illusions of Reality / Reality of Illusions".*

Photo by Christopher Agius Burke.
PAGE 12: *(TOP) Bea Szenfeld. (BOTTOM) "Shadow of a Bat" by Rob Elford.*
PAGE 16: *Elena Slivnyak.*
PAGE 298: *Olga Noronha. Photo by Andre Brito.*
FINAL PAGE: *Sasha Frovola. "Lyubolet". Inflatable latex sculpture and two aliens suits. Photo: Anna Pitich, 2008.*
BACK COVER: *Elena Slivnyak. Photo by Kristina Varaksina.*

SPECIAL THANKS:

Kazuma "Fuzzy" Mori, for his contributions to the Kansai Yamamoto story, and Masae Ueno, for additional English translation. Special thanks to Rodolphe Lachat of Cernunnos for giving us the extra time to do this special project correctly.

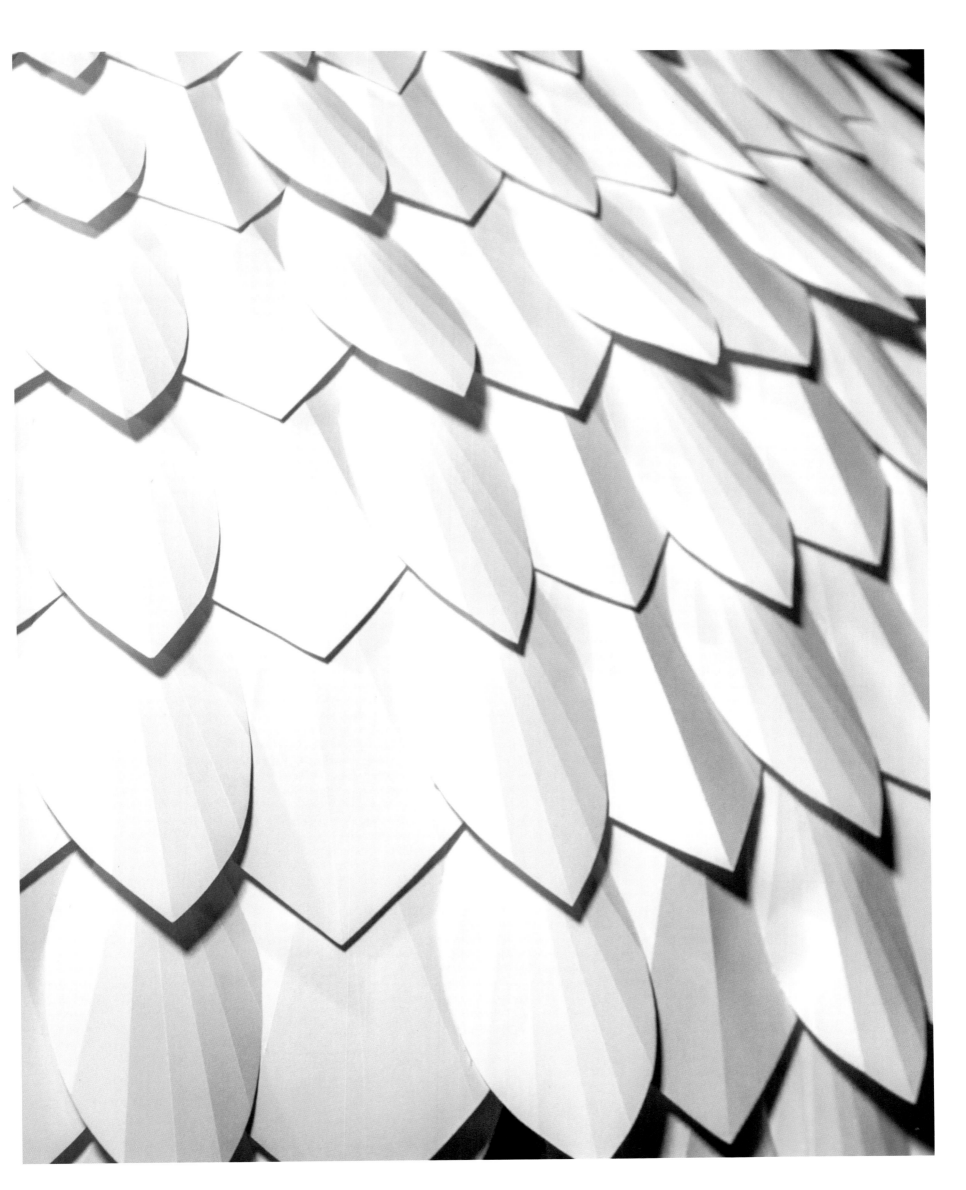

Hi-Fructose: New Contemporary Fashion
Hi-Fructose Founders/Editors In Chief:
Attaboy and Annie Owens

CERNUNNOS

First published in 2019 by CERNUNNOS
An imprint of Dargaud
57 rue Gaston Tessier
75019 Paris
www.cernunnospublishing.com
ISBN: 9782374950501

Director of publication: Rodolphe Lachat
Cernunnos logo design: Mark Ryden
Cover: Bea Szenfeld. Photo by Joel Rhodin.
Backcover: Elena Slivnyak.
Photo by Kristina Varaksina.
Dépôt legal: Janvier 2019
Printed in Spain by Industria Grafica Cayfo.